Unless You Become
As a Little Child

JOAN GALLI

CREATION HOUSE
H O U S E
A STRANG COMPANY

UNLESS YOU BECOME AS A LITTLE CHILD by Joan Galli
Published by Creation House
A Strang Company
600 Rinehart Road
Lake Mary, Florida 32746
www.creationhouse.com

Unless otherwise noted, all Scripture quotations are from the New King James Version of the Bible. Copyright © 1979, 1980, 1982 by Thomas Nelson, Inc., publishers. Used by permission.

Scripture quotations marked AMP are from the Amplified Bible. Old Testament copyright 1965, 1987 by the Zondervan Corporation. The Amplified New Testament copyright 1954, 1958, 1987 by the Lockman Foundation. Used by permission.

Scripture quotations marked NAS are from the New American Standard Bible. Copyright © 1960, 1962, 1963, 1968, 1971, 1972, 1973, 1975, 1977 by the Lockman Foundation. Used by permission. (www.Lockman.org)

The names of the living have been changed to protect their privacy.

Cover design by Popcorn Initiative

Library of Congress Control Number: 2005930416
International Standard Book Number: 1-59185-904-2

05 06 07 08 09— 987654321
Printed in the United States of America

This book is dedicated to the memory of our daughter

Mary Bernadette Galli
January 24, 1959 – January 7, 1961

And
To all who will become like little children
So as
To enter the kingdom of heaven

Acknowledgments

THIS BOOK IS A RESULT OF the enabling power of the Holy Spirit and the encouragement of family and friends.

I am most grateful to my son Jim and daughter-in-law Carol for their gift of a laptop computer and their insistence it be used to "Write your book, Mom."

A debt of gratitude is owed to my son Jerome for his patience and constant help in teaching me the wonders of a computer and also for his legal expertise.

I acknowledge the contagious enthusiasm and expert promotional advice from my son Peter. It was always an added blessing.

To my darling granddaughters, Julie and Katie, I have promised the very first copies of Grandma's book. Their love and support have been precious.

There is endless thanksgiving in my heart for the thirty-five and a half wonderful years with Oscar, my dear departed husband, without whom this book could never have been written.

I am extremely grateful to my faithful friend Ginny Sandis for her tireless efforts in editing and reediting this manuscript.

May God continue to pour out His abundant blessings through the power of His Holy Spirit!

Contents

Introduction

———◆———

BORN INTO A STRICT, IRISH CATHOLIC family, I had been taught the love of God and the power of prayer from early childhood. However, through the years, it was becoming increasingly more difficult to explain the deep yearning in my soul for "something more." After a move to California and through an unusual set of circumstances, I discovered there was another baptism known as the baptism of the Holy Spirit.

> For John truly baptized with water, but you shall be baptized with the Holy Spirit...you shall receive power when the Holy Spirit has come upon you; and you shall be witnesses to Me...to the end of the earth.
>
> —ACTS 1:5, 8

By God's grace, I experienced this baptism on July 20, 1971. It was then that the amazing realm of the supernatural began to unfold in my life.

Today, I stand in awe at what the third Person of the Trinity has taught, and daily continues to teach me through the Holy Scriptures. Revealing His book as the living Word, the author has brought me into a loving relationship with Him, my Savior. I have finally found the "something more" my heart had been longing for.

After the birth of our fourth child, surgery prevented my regular attendance at a Monday night prayer meeting. What appeared devastating to me at the time, turned out to be a great blessing, resulting in hundreds of prayer meetings held in our home. I hope to portray in the following pages some of the wonder, excitement, and miraculous events that occurred in those meetings and since my encounter with the Holy Spirit. Many of the teachings and experiences during those years still astound me. Most of all, I desire to continue working on my L.C. (Little Child), by becoming as trusting and teachable as a little child.

> Assuredly, I say to you, whoever does not receive the kingdom of God as a little child will by no means enter it.
>
> —Mark 10:15

I have written this book with the express purpose of giving all the glory to my heavenly Father for sending His Son Jesus to save me; and to Jesus for sending the Holy Spirit to indwell and inspire me.

My prayer is that you, the reader, have already experienced or soon will encounter the power of the Holy Spirit, the wonderful truth of His Word, and will also be astounded at His marvelous manifestations in your life.

Behold, I stand at the door and knock. If anyone hears My voice and opens the door, I will come in to him and dine with him, and he with Me.

—REVELATION 3:20

CHAPTER 1

A Move to Change Lives

—■◆■—

Monday of Thanksgiving week, in 1969, we moved into our home in sunny California following my husband's job transfer from Illinois. Our little family consisted of my husband, Oscar; twelve-year-old son, Jim; a Pekinese dog named Tiger; and me, six months pregnant.

God soon blessed us with another beautiful son whom we named Jerome Oscar. Due to stomach problems, our precious little boy cried constantly. Three doctors diagnosed his problem as pyloric stenosis, in which the opening to his stomach wasn't functioning properly; this caused projectile vomiting. The doctors all agreed he did not need surgery and would outgrow it in a month or two. The problem lasted for many months and became an extremely trying time in our lives; there was no reprieve from the baby's cries of pain. Night and day we paced the floor. Frequently, I would also be in tears as I tried to comfort our darling, suffering little baby.

Oscar put in long hours at his new job. No longer provided with a company car, he drove the family car to work. For the first time ever, I was confined to home. I worried about my husband working so hard and was concerned for our older son in a new school. Longing for the phone to ring and exhausted from lack of sleep, I felt forsaken; family and friends were now so far away. Enclosed backyards with vine-covered fences prevented even a glimpse of a neighbor. The California sun regularly disappeared behind rain clouds. The blessing of daily Mass was no longer an option and the many rosaries, litanies, and novenas seemed to fall on deaf ears. God also seemed to be very far away. There was a longing in my soul for "something more." We had prayed for years to be blessed with more children and were so grateful for God's recent blessing. Now, however, it was becoming increasingly difficult to reconcile my growing desperation in trying to comfort this beautiful, screaming baby.

In early spring, our little family was thrilled to join Oscar when he had meetings to attend in the Midwest. We were able to spend Easter and the following week with my parents. During this time, my father received word that his oldest brother, Jerome, a Trappist monk, had gone to heaven. Through his tears and with a trembling voice, dad read a letter from the dear monk who had been with Brother Jerome during their three-hour Good Friday service. He told how, at a quarter to three, Jerome folded his arms across his chest and "gave up the ghost." The brother shared the expressed longing in Jerome's heart for the privilege of dying on the same day as his Lord.

My thoughts went back to the times we had visited my uncle at the monastery. He was very thin, as a result of a life of fasting, and spoke in a whisper due to the many years of silence. The presence of Jesus in him lit up his stark surroundings. He was the most humble and holy man I had ever met. I remember he shared his longing for heaven and stressed the importance of a close walk each day with the Lord. He laughed and said we will no doubt have two big questions about our brothers and sisters in heaven: *How did YOU get here?* and *Where is HE?* He meant that we should expect some unexpected people to show up in heaven, and that we might be surprised at who is absent. God alone is the perfect Judge.

> Judge not, that you be not judged. For with what judgment you judge, you will be judged.
>
> —MATTHEW 7:1–2

> Not everyone who says to Me, "Lord, Lord," shall enter the kingdom of heaven, but he who does the will of My Father in heaven.
>
> —MATTHEW 7:21

One of the monks later wrote and shared that Jerome had memorized most of the New Testament and often spoke of his eagerness to be with Jesus. I had always written to Brother Jerome at Christmas and Easter, sending offerings for Masses and asking for his prayers. That Easter I had written about the birth of our second son, whom we named after him. Because Brother Jerome never read mail during Lent as an added sacrifice, he died not knowing about his namesake. Disappointed, I prayed about this and I had a strong sense that he already knew; the accompanying thought was that his namesake would someday speak forth the many things he had spent a lifetime of silence praying for.

> Precious in the sight of the LORD is the death of His saints.
>
> —PSALM 116:15

A few months later, my dear Methodist neighbor came to visit and brought a book she thought I would enjoy. It was *Catholic Pentecostals*, by Kevin Ranahan. She had heard it advertised on Christian radio and felt impressed to buy it for me. Years later, she confessed to being apprehensive in giving me that book, but felt the Lord leading her to do so. I thank God for her obedience. At first, because of my strict Catholic background, I placed the book on a shelf and wondered why a Protestant would be giving such a book to me. In a few days, curiosity got the better of me and I began to read a book that would change my life. For the first time, I learned about Catholics receiving the baptism of the Holy Spirit. Literally consuming the book, I realized this was what was missing in my life.

A new acquaintance from church stopped by one morning and noticed the book on my table. She had also read it and had recently experienced the baptism of the Holy Spirit. Realizing how eager I was for this experience, she and another lady took me to a Catholic home prayer group two days later. The meeting had been canceled, but twelve people showed up. I was a little uncomfortable at first; everyone prayed with eyes closed and upraised hands.

> I desire therefore that the men pray everywhere, lifting up holy hands.
>
> —1 TIMOTHY 2:8

However, the same sweet presence of the Lord was there that I had experienced when we visited my brother and uncle in the Trappist monastery. After beautiful singing, Scripture readings, and sharing, it was time for prayer. My friend announced that I would like to be prayed over for the Holy Spirit baptism. A chair was placed in the middle of the room for me. People gathered around and laid hands on my head and shoulders. Simple prayers were said asking Jesus to baptize me with His Holy Spirit. Immediately, I felt as though scales were pulled from my eyes and plugs removed from my ears. I heard people quoting from Matthew and John. I cannot describe the instant hunger I felt for God's Word. I've often said I would eat the Book with a spoon if I could. I was flooded with joy and love as I stood up and began hugging everyone with the love of the Lord.

My spiritual birthday was July 20, 1971. To my amazement, I later discovered in my Sunday missal, this day was also the feast day of St. Jerome Emilian. (The date has been changed on recent calendars.) Jerome was the name of our baby son and Emilia was the name of my mother-in-law. She resented the fact that her son did not marry a "nice Italian girl," and made life difficult for me. These were the two people in my life that caused me to seek the Lord with all my heart. Today, one of my favorite scriptures is:

> For I know the thoughts that I think toward you, says
> the LORD, thoughts of peace and not of evil, to give you
> a future and a hope.... And you will seek Me and find
> Me, when you search for Me with all your heart.
> —JEREMIAH 29:11, 13

After being prayed for I remember feeling as though I was floating on a cloud. Over and over I found myself uttering the phrase, "Praise You Father, Praise You Son, Praise You Holy Spirit, Three in One." "Praise the Lord" popped out of my mouth so often my husband was concerned that I sounded like a fanatic. He also was amazed that my favorite book had now become *The Good News for Modern Man.* Oscar recalled how he had always loved to read Scripture, especially the

Psalms. I only read the Bible during Lent, as a penance. It had previously been difficult for me to understand and even boring, but now, with the Author illuminating it, I could hardly put it down.

> All Scripture is given by inspiration of God, and is profitable for doctrine, for reproof, for correction, for instruction in righteousness.
>
> —2 TIMOTHY 3:16

Linda (one of the ladies that had taken me to be prayed over for the baptism) asked if I would like to join her in attending a prayer meeting at a Catholic Retreat Center. The meetings were held every Monday evening. My wonderful husband baby-sat and encouraged me to go; he realized how important this had become in my new walk with the Lord. Most of the people in attendance had received the baptism of the Holy Spirit. The spontaneous music was heavenly with its crescendos and decrescendos; it was as though an unseen conductor directed the beautiful blend of voices to begin and to cease simultaneously. I was thrilled to learn this was called "singing in the Spirit," better known as "worshiping in tongues."

> But the hour is coming, and now is, when the true worshipers will worship the Father in spirit and truth; for the Father is seeking such to worship Him. God is Spirit, and those who worship Him must worship in spirit and truth.
>
> —JOHN 4:23–24

The profound teachings at those meetings filled my heart with the truth of God's Word. I could listen to those humble men, so full of wisdom, for hours. What a surprise and shock it was to learn the speakers were Baptist, Pentecostal, and Lutheran, as well as Catholic. Gradually, I began to experience the meaning of one flock and one Shepherd and often repented of my narrow-mindedness in thinking somehow we Catholics had a corner on God.

> And other sheep I have which are not of this fold; them also I must bring, and they will hear My voice; and there will be one flock and one shepherd.
>
> —JOHN 10:16

> I do not pray for these alone, but also for those who will believe in Me through their word; that they all may be one, as You, Father, are in Me, and I in You; that they also may be one in Us, that the world may believe that You sent Me.
>
> —JOHN 17:20–21

Monday night prayer meetings became a highlight of the week. The longing in my soul for more of God was finally being met. Along with the inspirational teachings from God's Word and learning songs filled with Scripture came amazing manifestations of the Holy Spirit. On several occasions, during the service, there was an unmistakable scent of flowers. After the meetings, Linda's friend, Mary, who sat across the room, would ask if we had smelled the flowers. I would blurt out that it smelled like roses or lilacs or it was unrecognizable; sometimes Mary would say first what the scent was and it was always the same for both of us. My friend Linda never did experience this, but on one occasion, she also saw the girl's long hair in front of us moving, as though a breeze of the Holy Spirit was blowing, just before the heavenly scents came. This happened in the winter with doors and windows shut and no flowers in the room.

Prayer was always available following the meetings. One evening due to severe back pain, I went forward for prayer. Seating me in a chair, a lady on the prayer team took my feet in her hands; she said a simple prayer asking God to align my body in the name of Jesus. Instantly, I experienced a stretching in my right thigh as my friend noticed my leg move forward. I stood free from the back pain that had plagued me for years; it has not recurred in more than thirty years.

> And whatever you ask in My name, that I will do, that the Father may be glorified in the Son.
> —John 14:13

The baby still cried and solid food wouldn't stay down but there was a new grace and power to cling to.

> But you shall receive power when the Holy Spirit has come upon you…
> —Acts 1:8

My focus had changed from the problem to the answer, which I learned was to praise God in all things and for all things. I had joined the church choir and began to sing again.

> Praise the Lord! Sing to the Lord a new song, and His praise in the assembly of saints.
> —Psalm 149:1

Later that year, on a Monday night, the chapel at Vallombrosa Center was packed; there wasn't an empty seat. Many clergy, on retreat, had come to check out the prayer meeting. In spite of being a baby in the Spirit, I recognized from the beginning that something was wrong. A dark cloud hung over the room. The singing was flat, and the peace and joy that had always been there was absent. After a short while, the leader announced the need for prayer to dispel the spirits of doubt and unbelief. As the group began to intercede, a number of men in black rose to leave. I was saddened at the look of arrogance and disdain on many of the clergy's faces as they left the chapel. Soon, the meeting began to flow in the power of the Holy Spirit as usual. After the service, I asked a nun sitting next to me if she would like to go up for prayer for the baptism of the Holy Spirit. She gave me a disgusted look and stood up to leave. Two young priests, on the other side of her, had overheard my question and said they would like to receive this baptism. I walked to the front with them and rejoiced as I watched the humility with which they asked another priest to pray that Jesus would baptize them with His Holy Spirit. They were hospital chaplains from Texas and expressed warm gratitude for my encouragement to go for prayer.

God was answering Pope John the XXIII's prayer for a new Pentecost and fresh move of the Holy Spirit in the Catholic Church. One could attend a prayer meeting any night of the week. A wonderful little prayer meeting had begun in my church. Soon, however, it was moved to the library next door and then to a convent garage that had been converted into a hall. Many were shocked and hurt at the way the Holy Spirit was relegated to a basement, garage, or back room. The buzz seemed to be that Charismatics were too emotional and attracted kooks. A dear friend and I often laughed, commenting on the scripture that states, "But God has chosen the foolish things of the world to put to shame the wise" (1 Cor. 1:27). We gladly proclaimed our foolishness for Christ, vowing to pray even more diligently for our relatives and friends to experience more of Jesus through His Holy Spirit.

books, tapes, and letters to everyone I could think
them about the wonderful Holy Spirit. One of my
bridesmaids later told me she thought I had really flipped out
until she was at the hospital with a sick child and noticed *The
Good News For Modern Man* in the waiting room. Recalling I
had suggested she read it, she opened the book and was surprised to find written on the inside cover: "This is for you, please
take it." She did take it and began to discover the truth of God's
Word. Both she and her husband also had a mighty encounter
with the Holy Spirit. They have since been actively spreading
the good news in their parish and town for many years.

My dear friend, Linda, who took me to my first prayer
meeting, became my mentor in the things of the Lord. I was
unaware of all the wonderful Christian radio and TV pro-
grams. She kept me informed about the various seminars and
retreats and would bring back detailed notes and full reports
from conferences she had attended at Notre Dame, Kansas
City, Rome, and even Jerusalem.

During a prayer meeting I enthusiastically shared a teaching I had received that week while I was praying. I had been
impressed that we were all called to be like John the Baptist,
preparing the way for the Second Coming of the Lord. Many
times when I looked at the clock it was either 3:30 a.m. or
3:30 p.m. The accompanying thought was that it must always
be "John 3:30 time." Checking my Bible, I was blessed to
discover that John the Baptist said, "He must increase, but
I must decrease" (John 3:30). I then asked Linda to give us
some highlights from the retreat she had just come from. She
laughed and said the Lord had given me the very teaching
about John the Baptist that she had planned to share.

Jesus Christ is the same yesterday, today, and forever.
—HEBREWS 13:8

My family greatly loved Linda and considered her to be a true saint of God. She would help anyone at any time and was always full of laughter and a kind word. One day she came with *The New American Bible* and informed me I needed to really grow in the Lord by reading the whole book. Linda explained her excitement and wonder at reading the many prophecies from the Old Testament that were fulfilled in Jesus' coming in the New Testament. I knew she was right in encouraging me to study the whole book. After reading dozens of books detailing others' testimonies, I had been questioning God about how to get my own testimony. Always the same answer seemed to be, "Pray often and study My Word, then I will take care of your testimony." Up to that time, I had been reading only the New Testament. I was still hesitant to read the Old Testament and fought it for months, thinking I didn't have time. Picking up a tract someone had given me, I was greatly convicted when I read the following line at the bottom of the tract: "This selection of Holy Scripture is a part of the Old Testament. We urge you next to read the entire Bible." With that admonition, I began to read: "In the beginning..." I continue to read through God's Holy Word each year and am most grateful for the testimony He is now developing in me as I study His *entire* book.

My mentor, Linda, also introduced me to monthly Saturday morning breakfast meetings. The man who ran the book table had been healed of a back injury. He hauled many heavy boxes of books each month and gave God the glory for his healing. Linda and I were some of his best customers. The speakers were full to overflowing with the Holy Spirit, blessing everyone with gems from God's Word. Afterward, there was always prayer available from the guest speaker. I was never shy about getting in a prayer line for more of the Lord's blessings. After one meeting, the speaker, a Baptist preacher, and his wife prayed over me. During prayer, she saw a ball of fire enter me and at that moment he announced the Lord had just infused me with the gifts of joy and encouragement. This has been a cause for my giving thanks and glory to God, as over the years many have commented on the evidence of these two gifts in my life. I later heard that the "J" in *joy* should be for *Jesus*, the "O" for *others*, and the "Y" for *you*. There is so much available to God's children, but "you do not have because you do not ask" (James 4:2).

Linda and I frequently would attend a healing Mass, and afterward get in line to be prayed for. One night, I decided to ask prayer for my feet, since they had bothered me for as long as I could remember. I was in constant pain from bone spurs on the bottoms of my heels. Years ago, I had gone to a foot doctor in the Midwest. The x-rays revealed the bone spurs. My dad and I had the same problem and were both fitted with special shoe pads to relieve the pain. The doctor did not recommend surgery, stating the spurs usually grew back. Walking or standing for any length of time had become extremely painful. All of my shoes had holes dug into the heels from the bone spurs. The lady that prayed for me had been healed of this very thing, and had great faith for my healing. Two or three days after being prayed for, it dawned on me I no longer had any pain. Thirty years later, I'm still thanking the Great Physician for my healing. The lady who prayed over me had the same last name as the foot doctor. I like to call this a divine coincidence.

He sent His word and healed them, and delivered them from their destructions.

—Psalm 107:20

Because my mother and dad were both the youngest of nine children, this gave me a great opportunity to write and share the Lord with elderly uncles and aunts. I usually added the following prayer on a get-well card stating how much it had blessed me: "Lord Jesus, please forgive me for every sin I have ever committed. I invite you to come into my heart as my Lord and Savior; I receive Your free gift of salvation. Please fill me with Your Holy Spirit and I will serve you all the days of my life." With childlike faith I prayed trusting God for their salvation.

> Whoever calls on the name of the Lord shall be saved.
> —ROMANS 10:13

One of the greatest longings in my heart is to meet every relative, friend, and child that I have ever taught, in heaven.

> Let not your heart be troubled; you believe in God, believe also in Me. In My Father's house are many mansions; if it were not so, I would have told you. I go to prepare a place for you.... I will come again and receive you to Myself; that where I am, there you may be also.
> —JOHN 14:1–3

CHAPTER 2

Added Blessings

————•◆•————

W E WERE BLESSED WITH A FULL house one Christmas when my younger brother, his wife, and four little ones came from Iowa to visit. Oscar's mother, Emilia, known as Nona to the children, was also visiting from Chicago. The cousins had a great time together and there was much discussion among the adults about the Holy Spirit, at least on my part. After returning home, my brother called to say my frequent expression of "Praise the Lord" was annoying, but he could see I had something special. My sister-in-law remembered my saying, "Jesus stands knocking at the door of our hearts, and if we open, He will come in." The Bible says, "Behold, I stand at the door and knock. If anyone hears My voice and opens the door, I will come in to him" (Rev. 3:20). After going home, she had been awakened during the night by a bright light at the foot of the bed. The above verse immediately came to her mind. She asked Jesus into her heart and had a beautiful encounter with Him. Later, her brother and a priest friend prayed for my brother, Bill, who also received the baptism of the Holy Spirit.

My parents used to visit from Iowa during the winter months to escape the snow and cold weather of the Midwest. A growing concern of my father was that I sounded like a Protestant, due to my frequently quoting from the Bible. He constantly checked to see if I was reading the Catholic version. We had ongoing and sometimes heated discussions until Mother would suggest we change the subject. I will never forget the look of horror and disbelief on their faces when I informed them Jesus wasn't Catholic. I reminded them He was a Jew, jokingly remarking that Dad no doubt thought He was Irish Catholic, to which he sheepishly agreed. Mother was much more open to God's Word and had a marvelous encounter with the Holy Spirit. Dad was more comfortable checking everything out with my older brother, who had spent six years in a Trappist monastery studying for the priesthood. Sadly, he frequently scoffed at my Bible reading which added to Dad's confusion. It was frustrating to realize, in spite of how prayerful and holy Dad was, he had been taught to trust in his tradition rather than in God's Holy Word: "For laying aside the commandment of God, you hold the tradition of men" (Mark 7:8). He had a difficult time reading the Bible, yet he would spend hours on his rote prayers. The Bible says, "And when you pray, do not use vain repetitions" (Matt. 6:7). I knew how much God loved this obedient and faithful servant, but always felt He had so much more for my wonderful father, if only he was more open to the truth of God's Word.

Often in my prayer time, the thought would come, "It is my desire for you to have one more child." I usually dismissed it thinking I must be crazy to even consider such a thing now that our two-year-old was so active. When the above thought became more frequent during prayer, I decided to inform my husband. Oscar's reaction matched mine, recalling the fact that we were getting too old to raise another little one and what if we had a "screamer" again? After much prayer, we discarded the calendar and soon were expecting another blessed event. I had forgotten the doctor's warning, after our third child, of no more pregnancies or I would face having the varicose veins in my leg stripped. Early in this pregnancy, it occurred to me that I never had morning sickness, and the veins that caused such agonizing pain during the previous pregnancy no longer pulsed and burned. Little by little, I was learning to enjoy the blessings of obedience.

> And all these blessings shall come upon you and overtake you, because you obey the voice of the LORD your God.
> —DEUTERONOMY 28:2

One day, a call came from a doctor in Chicago informing us that Oscar's mother had suffered a massive heart attack with a 50 percent chance of survival. She was a widow and Oscar an only child; we made immediate plans to go to her. Arriving at the hospital, Oscar and I were taken to the intensive care unit where we could see Emilia's heart monitor. I stared at the monitor silently seeking God as to whether she was ready to be with Him. The answer seemed to be in the negative. As I prayed with all my heart, it was as though a voice on my left kept urging me to just let her go, reminding me of how she resented me and where she would most likely live. A voice on my right strongly impressed me that she was not ready to meet her Maker, encouraging me to intercede for her and my prayers would be heard. The taunting voice on my left continued to bombard my mind with the thought that she could live to be one hundred, making my life miserable. I suddenly felt in the middle of a spiritual battle for her eternal destiny. With great conviction, I quietly prayed, begging the Lord that she not be lost and to please save her soul, no matter what. The second I uttered that prayer, her heart began a regular rhythm on the monitor. Oscar and I burst into tears of relief and thanksgiving. I stood in awe at the power of simple, heartfelt prayers, for I knew Oscar was agonizing in prayer over his mother also.

> Have faith in God. For assuredly, I say to you, whoever says to this mountain, 'Be removed and be cast into the sea,' and does not doubt in his heart, but believes that those things he says will be done, he will have whatever he says. Therefore I say to you, whatever things you ask when you pray, believe that you receive them, and you will have them.
>
> —Mark 11:22–24

> Praise the Lord! I will praise the Lord with my whole heart.
>
> —Psalm 111:1

We packed and shipped many of Emilia's things to the West Coast. She had always promised to move near us and now this was a must. Nona was improving steadily; the doctor said Oscar could fly back and bring her to our home in a few weeks. I'll never forget the day she arrived. She had been through much suffering and the compassion of the Lord flooded over me when I saw her. The years of her negative comments vanished as I recalled our thanksgiving to God for hearing and answering our sincere prayers, several weeks earlier.

Caring for Nona became very difficult. As I continually helped lift her from the bed, couch, and chair, I experienced stomach pain and bleeding, which caused great concern for the new life God was forming in me.

> For You formed my inward parts; you covered me in my mother's womb. I will praise You, for I am fearfully and wonderfully made.
>
> —PSALM 139:13–14

Oscar and I went to talk with Mother Superior at a lovely retirement home nearby. She recognized me from morning Mass attendance in their chapel. We shared how much we wanted another child and the problem we were having. Mother Superior showed us the long list of names waiting to enter; then she began to write Emilia's name at the top, stating she would not want anything to happen to this new life. We left there hand-in-hand thanking God for more answered prayer. Nona was okay with going to such a nice place; she, too, was very concerned for the much-anticipated new arrival.

Seeing my mother-in-law in the front row at morning Mass at the Villa, I was overcome with emotion and could not keep the tears back. Nona had been a CEO—Christmas and Easter Only—Catholic but after twenty-one years of intercession for her, there she was receiving communion. The wonderful Italian chaplain greatly blessed her and the darling nuns gave her excellent care.

Out of the blue, my uncle, Father Edward, T.O.R., called saying he was in California and was coming for a visit. We were thrilled because he was a laugh a minute. He had traveled the world but had never been to the Golden State. He especially enjoyed visiting San Francisco; being a Franciscan, he naturally commented on the city being named after good St. Francis. Each morning, he said Mass at the Villa where Nona was. Afterward, I would fix his breakfast, and we would have lengthy discussions about the Bible until lunch and then again until dinner. I showed him about the baptism of the Holy Spirit in all four Gospels and also in the Acts of the Apostles. (See Matthew 3:11; Mark 1:8; Luke 3:16; John 1:33; and Acts 1:5.) He kept repeating that my parents had me baptized as an infant. I continued to stress there was another baptism available for the asking.

> Jesus answered, "Most assuredly, I say to you, unless one is born of water and the Spirit, he cannot enter the kingdom of God. That which is born of the flesh is flesh, and that which is born of the Spirit is spirit. Do not marvel that I said to you, 'You must be born again.'"
>
> —JOHN 3:5–7

After four days of ongoing discussion about God's Word, with tears in his eyes, he remarked it didn't seem fair that I was just a housewife and appeared to know God better than he who had given his life to serve Him.

> So He said to them, "Assuredly, I say to you, there is no one who has left house or parents…for the sake of the kingdom of God, who shall not receive many times more in this present time, and in the age to come eternal life"
>
> —LUKE 18:29–30

It was unbelievably disappointing to observe this brilliant man, who had studied four years in Rome and was ordained there, had a Doctorate of Divinity, and had been president of a university, not grasping a simple truth from God's Word. I accused my dad of arranging that trip for his favorite brother to straighten out his Protestant-sounding daughter, but he always, laughingly, denied it.

The birth of another baby was an extra special miracle of God, since it was the first time my husband was allowed to be in the delivery room with me. We were hoping God would bless us with a girl to help fill the void after our little Mary Bernadette's death. We even had two sets of names picked out; both sets of names were amazingly later used for our two granddaughters. When the doctor announced that the plumbing was on the outside, we all laughed and rejoiced over a third beautiful, healthy boy. Both Oscar and I were crying tears of joy; the doctor was also teary-eyed at our happiness. A rainbow filled the window as I was brought back to my room. We couldn't stop praising and thanking God for blessing us with another child. Together, we agreed his name should be Peter Francis, after my father. The following day, a cleaning lady said she was trying to locate the older couple that was so happy at the birth of their baby. Realizing her search had ended, she laughed and remarked she had seldom seen such a happy couple and assumed it was our first child.

Several months after having the baby, I went to the doctor for a checkup. He discovered fibroid tumors and encouraged me to schedule a hysterectomy. I hated to tell my husband since I was secretly still hoping for a girl. I did break the bad news and, immediately, Oscar picked up the phone and insisted I call the doctor right back. Understandably, all he could think of was possibly trying to raise a teenager, a toddler and a new baby, without their mother.

Following the surgery, there was much happiness in my coming home from the hospital. I was greeted with a big "welcome home" sign and hugs and kisses galore from my guys. However, I soon felt overwhelmed. The baby was crying, but the doctor had forbidden me to lift him after surgery, which broke my heart. The house was in total disarray, my poor husband was frazzled, and the toddler and teen both needed Mom's attention. My wonderful spouse got me settled into bed and went to tend to our three sons.

Alone in the darkened room, I began to cry out to the Lord. While praying, I had a mental picture of myself standing at the base of a mountain. Its pink, shiny surface reminded me of my grandmother's granite headstone. I couldn't see over or around it and I had a feeling of complete helplessness. I continued to pray and suddenly an archway opened up before me. Looking through it, I saw clear, placid water, with little sailboats going toward a white lighthouse in the distance. A wonderful calm and peace came over me, along with a knowing that my heavenly Father was very much in charge. One day I would understand the meaning of what I had just experienced.

> Therefore do not worry about tomorrow... Sufficient for the day is its own trouble.
>
> —Matthew 6:34

One Sunday, Nona had come for dinner and was sitting in the front room when I heard her moan. I ran to her just as her eyes rolled back and she slumped to one side turning a grayish color. In my mind I heard, "Rebuke the spirit of death." I shouted, "Spirit of death, I rebuke you and command you to loose Emilia, in the name of Jesus Christ!" Immediately, she straightened up and looked at me. Her color was returning to normal once again. Oscar was dialing 911. The paramedics arrived shortly and determined she had suffered a heart attack.

This would be her second time to be hospitalized and then sent to a nursing home to recover while she was bedridden. At that time, the retirement home could only accommodate ambulatory residents. Nona hated spending a couple of weeks in the nursing home, but it was our only recourse.

A few months later, Emilia had another heart attack and was once again in the hospital. She had diabetes and a failed kidney. Oscar and I took turns visiting Nona daily at mealtime to try to get her to eat. I had caught a cold and was afraid of passing it on, so I missed seeing her for a few days.

While praying for Emilia one evening, I smelled a heavenly scent of roses. Since it was the end of March and raining outside, there was no evidence of earthly flowers. I asked God what it meant. I opened my *Good News Bible* and began to read:[1]

> But thanks be to God! For in union with Christ we are always led by God as prisoners in Christ's victory procession. God uses us to make the knowledge about Christ spread everywhere like a sweet fragrance. For we are like a sweet-smelling incense offered by Christ to God, which spreads among those who are being saved and those who are being lost. For those who are being lost, it is a deadly stench that kills; but for those who are being saved, it is a fragrance that brings life. Who, then, is capable for such a task? We are not like so many others, who handle God's message as if it were cheap merchandise; but because God has sent us, we speak with sincerity in his presence, as servants of Christ.
> —2 CORINTHIANS 2:14–17

I then noticed the heading which read, "Victory through Christ." I felt God was letting me know Nona was ready to meet Him.

A few days later, a call came from Emilia's doctor. He said since there was nothing more they could do for her, she was being sent back to the nursing home. I hung up the phone and got on my knees asking God to please ease Nona's suffering and take her to heaven, if she was ready. I knew how furious she would be to wake up, back in that facility. Shortly, the phone rang again, and the doctor said when they went to get her for the ambulance, she had expired. I called Oscar at work and we cried together, trusting his mother was safely home. He remarked how good God was to not let her wake up once again in the nursing home. It was April 4, 1974; I then recalled it had been nine months since our loving heavenly Father had answered our prayers that day in the intensive care unit.

Call to Me, and I will answer you...

—Jeremiah 33:3

CHAPTER 3

Love and Praise Days

⸺◆⸺

D<small>UE TO MY RECENT SURGERY, ATTENDING</small> the local Monday night prayer meeting was no longer an option. Bernadine called to tell me I was missed and that several were wondering if they could bring a prayer meeting to me; I was thrilled at the thought. Since my encounter with the Holy Spirit, there had always been a desire in my heart to have a meeting in our home. We agreed Thursday afternoon would be a good time to meet, and thus began one of the most interesting and fulfilling adventures of my life.

We had just celebrated the baby turning one year old when our first meeting was held. Four of us gathered around our kitchen table. One of the ladies read:

> Whenever you come together, each of you has a psalm, has a teaching, has a tongue, has a revelation, has an interpretation. Let all things be done for edification.
> —1 C<small>ORINTHIANS</small> 14:26

This became the format: along with many praise songs we would pray for each other's needs, share exciting answers to prayer, and enjoy sweet fellowship over coffee. Little did I realize that that was the beginning of hundreds of meetings to be held in our home. Every Thursday for the next nine and a half years, with very few exceptions, this faithful group met to praise the Lord and learn from His Word.

Each week, another lady or two joined us, in spite of the fact that it was never advertised. Someone remarked we were hand-picked by the Lord when He saw how eager we were for more of Him. Outgrowing the kitchen table by the third week, we moved to the front room. We then expanded from one row of chairs to two rows and, occasionally, when a guest speaker was invited, the room was filled with over forty people.

Since no one felt qualified to run the meeting, we all agreed that the Holy Spirit would direct. By summer that year, a schoolteacher was able to attend. After the meeting she questioned the group regarding the leader. She suggested everyone pray about this during the coming week, adding that she felt that I was to lead. I remember being upset at her suggestion since I cleaned the house, set up the chairs, made the coffee, had numerous phone calls, fed the little boys, got the baby down for a nap and didn't want the responsibility of also leading the meetings. After the meeting, I went to my prayer closet (the bathroom), got on my knees, and talked to the Lord about this. I asked Him, as I frequently did, to please speak through His Word.

After spending time in prayer, I opened my Bible expecting to receive an answer. It fell open to the book of Jonah. Familiar with the story, I felt that didn't apply. Closing the book, I prayed longer and opened the Bible a second time;

to my amazement I was looking at the story of Jonah once again. This was very puzzling. I had tightly closed the Bible, there was no marker in it, and Jonah is such a small book to open to, especially twice in a row. I read the four short chapters and decided if God was speaking through this, I had better obey. (I was not eager for a whale ride.) Later that day, our five-year-old brought in the mail and the magazine on top had "Jonah" in large letters written across the cover. A shudder went through me as I quietly said, "Yes, Lord, if this is what You want, I will, with Your help, become the leader." The following week, the group unanimously agreed I was to be the official leader. I was most grateful for the unusual preparation. The psalmist says, "Direct my steps by Your word, and let no iniquity have dominion over me" (Ps. 119:133). I was still experiencing apprehension about leading the group. This feeling intensified when I read verses like: "My brethren, let not many of you become teachers, knowing that we shall receive a stricter judgment" (James 3:1). Spending time in prayer and begging the Holy Spirit for help, I was comforted by reading:

> But sanctify the Lord God in your hearts, and always be ready to give a defense to everyone who asks you a reason for the hope that is in you, with meekness and fear.
>
> —1 PETER 3:15

> Let the word of Christ dwell in you richly in all wisdom, teaching and admonishing one another in psalms and hymns and spiritual songs, singing with grace in your hearts to the Lord.
>
> —COLOSSIANS 3:16

A strong admonition then came, in my spirit, to study and memorize God's Word so as to give it forth, and He would watch over His Word to perform it, as is stated in Isaiah 55:11. I just needed to obey, get my *self* out of the way, and let God have His way with this little group.

Now that we had a designated leader, we needed a name for our gathering. Suggestions were made, and "Love and Praise Prayer Group" was decided upon. This seemed to fulfill Jesus' great commandment to love God above all things and our neighbor as ourselves. (See Matthew 22:36–39.)

Beginning with the first meeting, there was an ongoing excitement and anticipation as to what the Holy Spirit would teach us. Everyone that came was seeking more of Jesus. The majority of the people attending had received the Holy Spirit baptism so unity, which only the Holy Spirit brings, was present each week. Prayer was always available after the meetings for anyone in need. The faith of each attendee was increasing weekly as we studied God's Word and began to believe and act upon it.

> So then faith comes by hearing, and hearing by the word of God.
> —ROMANS 10:17

A member named Eileen asked for prayer and believed God could work a miracle. Her doctor had discovered she had kidney stones and recommended surgery. We gathered around and anointed her with oil like we had read in James 5:14–15. With the hearts and faith of little children, we prayed asking God to dissolve the stones, trusting that nothing was impossible for Him.

> Is anything too hard for the LORD?
> —GENESIS 18:14

The following week, Eileen was bubbling over with excitement. She could hardly wait to share about going back to her doctor and asking for another x-ray, since she was no longer in pain. Three additional x-rays showed no trace of the stones. The doctor was baffled; he continued to study the original x-ray remarking she had to have passed the stones. She proceeded to tell him about being prayed over and all the pain leaving. With joyous laughter, she shared his look of disbelief on hearing such a thing. His nurse later confided he had become more frustrated with each x-ray. Eileen has since gone to heaven; to my knowledge, she never again was troubled with kidney stones.

> To another faith by the same Spirit, to another gifts of healing by the same Spirit.
> —1 CORINTHIANS 12:9

Pam, a dedicated member, shared how she almost didn't join us one Thursday, due to being in misery from allergies. Her eyes were nearly swollen shut and her sinuses were draining. During the meeting, someone had a word of knowledge that the Lord was healing allergies. Instantly, she felt a shrinking in the sinuses and her eyes stopped itching. She no longer needed the nine allergy shots she was to receive each week and has remained healed for over twenty-five years. Pam was so encouraged over that healing that she had faith to receive prayer for her bad back, which was also healed.

A little nun came to be prayed over for severe back pain. She called later, thanking and praising God that after many years, she was now pain-free.

A prayerful lady named Mary was healed of ovarian cancer. She had had prayer at our meeting, and had attended several other prayer meetings where she received additional prayer.

Lisa had smoked two and a half packs of cigarettes a day for twenty-five years and wanted prayer to be rid of her addiction. Upon hearing this, many of us gathered after a meeting to pray and ask God to set her free, in the name of His Son, Jesus. While we were praying, I had a mental picture of a flesh-colored hand moving across her black lungs. The hand turned black as the lungs turned pink. That instant, someone said they felt as though God was wiping her lungs clean with His hand. I remember excitedly shouting that was exactly what I had been seeing. Needless to say, we praised God for His marvelous manifestation. From that moment on, her desire for cigarettes left; she hasn't had one in over twenty years.

> But the manifestation of the Spirit is given to each one for the profit of all: for to one is given the word of wisdom through the Spirit, to another the word of knowledge through the same Spirit.
> —1 CORINTHIANS 12:7–8

One dear lady that faithfully attended Love and Praise asked for prayer for her husband who had begun to gamble. Their children had given them a weekend in Reno for their twenty-fifth wedding anniversary. When trying his luck at gambling, her husband had a real winning streak and then began to go back every chance he got. Little by little, he started to lose, but was positive he'd hit it big the next time. Breaking down in tears, she shared how he would get his paycheck and not even go home for his toothbrush; instead he headed straight to Reno. They had a large family with several children still at home. The prayer group collected funds to help with food. It wasn't long before they lost everything, including their lovely home with a swimming pool. Finally, this godly woman talked her husband into going for prayer. He did have an encounter with Jesus and then went for counseling. Later, the family moved to another state to start over. This was a painful lesson none of us could forget. Sadly, we watched the heartbreak and destruction caused by this addiction.

> The thief does not come except to steal, and to kill, and to destroy. I have come that they may have life, and that they may have it more abundantly.
>
> —JOHN 10:10

We were very encouraged however, to observe the power of persistent prayer in overcoming the enemy, and also to see God's restoration of a broken household.

> So I will restore to you the years that the swarming locust has eaten...You shall eat in plenty and be satisfied, and praise the name of the LORD your God.
>
> —JOEL 2:25–26

Nellie met a lady named Ila at church and invited her to the prayer meeting. Ila now credits the Lord she met at the Love and Praise meeting with saving her life. She had been seeing a doctor due to severe headaches, was unable to sleep, and had become so nervous she could no longer drive. For five years she had been "emotionally tortured" over the suicide of her dear mother. Blaming herself, she wondered if she could have done anything to prevent it; in severe depression, Ila had lost the desire to live. She was prayed over and received a number of healings. Someone had a word of knowledge regarding her mother that totally set her free. Ila said she felt deliverance and peace for the first time. She was given a Bible and later told me how blessed she was when she opened it and began to read:

Come to Me, all you who labor and are heavy laden, and I will give you rest. Take My yoke upon you and learn from Me, for I am gentle and lowly in heart, and you will find rest for your souls.

—Matthew 11:28–29

This wonderful sister was gifted with a true servant's heart. God seemed to reward her numerous acts of kindness, by blessing her with the writing of beautiful poetry and then with the gift of painting. Today, Ila is being used to bless many with her newly-discovered talents, and gives all the glory to her wonderful Savior. Recently, she ministered to a neighbor who had also experienced suicide in his family. What the enemy of our soul means for evil, our heavenly Father turns for good, if we trust Him.

Blessed be the God and Father of our Lord Jesus Christ, the Father of mercies and God of all comfort, who comforts us in all our tribulation, that we may be able to comfort those who are in any trouble, with the comfort with which we ourselves are comforted by God.

—2 Corinthians 1:3–4

Due to the fact that we met on Thursday afternoons, very few men attended Love and Praise. We did have a fascinating, retired judge from Hungary that frequently came. He loved God with all his heart and blessed us with his stories and prayers.

Another man seldom came to the Thursday meetings, but usually caused quite a stir when he did attend. In spite of having such a heart for the Lord, he annoyed everyone with his incessant preaching and advice. I was approached by two members after a particular meeting; they begged me to please talk with him to try and quiet him. I suggested the three of us pray right then, which we did, for the Holy Spirit to gently convict him.

> Again I say to you that if two of you agree on earth concerning anything that they ask, it will be done for them by My Father in heaven.
> —Matthew 18:19

The following week, before the meeting, he stopped to drop off literature and ads for other meetings. He then proceeded to tell me about a dream he had had during the week. In the dream, he was walking in front of Jesus; Jesus told him how much He loved him, but that he frequently was in His way. With tears welling up in his eyes, he admitted to having no idea of such a thing, saying he never, ever wanted to be in the Lord's way. I was sad for him, but also felt great relief on hearing how lovingly Abba Father dealt with this problem. I could hardly wait to tell my friends how beautifully our prayer had been answered.

> Ask, and it will be given to you...
> —Matthew 7:7

The majority of the Love and Praise Group was Catholic, representing eight or ten churches in the area. Over the years, we had Methodists, Lutherans, Presbyterians, and even an elderly little Pentecostal lady named Eunice, who amazed everyone with her knowledge of God's Word. While praying in the Spirit during one of the meetings, I had a mental picture of Eunice poking her head through the clouds; her face began to glow at what she was seeing. Afterward, I shared this with another member asking what she thought it meant. Together we felt perhaps God was planning to call her home soon. About two weeks later, I received a call that Eunice's son had found her in her bed, asleep forever. I love the verse: "Precious in the sight of the Lord is the death of His saints" (Ps. 116:15). This humble soul had been wonderfully used to inspire and bless our group. We all missed her but rejoiced at the thought of the great reward she must be enjoying.

An interesting thing happened with one lady who began coming to the meetings at the invitation of a friend. She remarked that she wanted what everyone else had. We asked if she would like prayer, and she agreed. The next week, she returned requesting more prayer, adding that something was still missing. When praying for her, someone felt she was holding on to false doctrine, but hesitated to say it. By asking her several questions, we discovered she believed in reincarnation. Bibles in hand, we read: "And as it is appointed for men to die once, but after this the judgment" (Heb. 9:27). She also thought there were many ways to heaven and refused to believe Jesus was the only provision God had made. Someone then read John 14:6, where Jesus told Thomas, "I am the way, the truth, and the life. No one comes to the Father except through Me." Also we shared: "For there is one God and one Mediator between God and men, the Man Christ Jesus, who gave Himself a ransom for all" (1 Tim. 2:5–6). God's Word was given in love, but she could not reconcile to this and stopped coming. Many prayers have been said for the Holy Spirit to lead this dear soul to the truth that Jesus is the only provision God has made for the salvation of mankind.

> For God so loved the world that He gave His only begotten Son, that whoever believes in Him should not perish but have everlasting life.
>
> —JOHN 3:16

A sweet little lady, that seldom attended the Group, informed me she was going to take classes in Buddhism. I was concerned that she was not grounded enough in the truth of God's Word to discern what she would be learning. As leader of the group, I felt very responsible to point people to Jesus and away from false gods, in obedience to the first commandment.

> I am the LORD your God, who brought you out of the land of Egypt, out of the house of bondage. You shall have no other gods before Me.
> —EXODUS 20:2–3

One of my most earnest prayers was that I would not be misled, or ever be used to mislead anyone. I could not stop praying for this lady, even when I was busy packing for a family vacation. Finally, I sat down and began to intercede for her. I then had a mental picture of a hummingbird flying toward a beautiful, open, pink hibiscus flower for its food. Instead of going to the flower, it turned aside to a dead tree stump where its long beak became caught; with wings fluttering its little body went limp against the dry wood. Alarmed by this pathetic scene, I asked the Holy Spirit to please show me its meaning. The immediate thought was: the beautiful flower represented God's truth bringing life, and the dead tree, the false religion that would bring death. I called to tell her I had been praying for her, which seemed to irritate her; when she asked why the prayers, I shared the above. She did not receive what I told her, which saddened me, but I felt I had obeyed the Holy Spirit's warning and was reminded of the following scripture:

> But when I speak with you, I will open your mouth, and you shall say to them, 'Thus says the Lord GOD,'

He who hears, let him hear; and he who refuses, let him refuse...

—Ezekiel 3:27

Donna, a member of our Thursday Group, called asking about a form of meditation that I was not familiar with. I suggested we pray for the Holy Spirit to lead us in His truth regarding it for "when He, the Spirit of truth, has come, He will guide you into all truth" (John 16:13). I expressed my very next thought that if we meditated on God's Word day and night, as His Word directs, that would leave no room for other types of meditation. The Bibles says, "Blessed is the man who walks not in the counsel of the ungodly... But his delight is in the law of the Lord, and in His law he meditates day and night" (Ps. 1:1–2). An answer from God's Holy Word totally satisfied Donna's open and obedient spirit; she hung up the phone praising God for His answer.

Oh, how I love Your law! It is my meditation all the day.
Your word is a lamp to my feet and a light to my path.

—Psalm 119: 97, 105

The phone rang constantly. In spite of the busy-ness and sometimes the frustrations of everyday life, I usually managed to answer with a cheery "hello." On one occasion, I overheard our six-year-old tell his baby brother, "That is Mommy's telephone voice." (This occurred after having just reprimanded them for something.) I remember checking in with the Lord to see if I was neglecting my family because of the prayer meeting; I also prayed with my husband regarding it. He was amused that I was concerned about neglecting our family, and lovingly affirmed my dedication to him and our three sons. Oscar could see how fulfilling the prayer group was.

He remarked about how he loved the feel of the house after a meeting, which I recognized as the lingering presence of the Lord. Likewise, a missionary from India used to say she felt she should remove her shoes when entering the meetings, due to the strong presence of the Holy Spirit.

Oscar did express concern that I was taking on problems from some members in the group, reminding me of the suicide of another prayer group leader. I confessed I had been having headaches and, after checking with the Lord, had the feeling He was displeased with me. Alarmed at what I could be doing wrong, I continued praying. Suddenly, the thought came to me that I was trying to play God. I was horrified and continued to pray, asking for His understanding. I was impressed to call a member of the prayer group and have her pray with me. I repented of taking on the group's many problems, instead of releasing them to the Lord and trusting Him with the outcome. As I obeyed, the headaches left immediately, never to return. This scripture came to mind:

> Come to Me, all you who labor and are heavy laden, and I will give you rest. Take My yoke upon you and learn from Me, for I am gentle and lowly in heart, and you will find rest for your souls. For My yoke is easy and My burden is light.
> —MATTHEW 11:28–30

What a gentle and powerful lesson I had learned. After sharing this, my dear, protective husband just shook his head as he heaved a sigh of relief.

Pam, a special friend and loyal member of the Love and Praise Prayer Group, stopped one morning to see if I'd like to accompany her to a local Bible study; babysitting was even provided. I was learning to do nothing without first praying about it so I told her I would let her know. In my prayer time, I asked the Lord for His direction regarding this study. To my surprise, a question came to mind asking why I would seek the living among the dead. Confused, I prayed more and the same thought kept returning. I called my friend to tell her I couldn't make it, giving no further explanation.

After several weeks, Pam popped in to say she wasn't getting a lot out of the Bible Study, in which they were studying Acts of the Apostles. She said the teacher and others in the class believed that the manifestations of the Spirit described in Acts were not relevant for today. Pam felt the Bible study was just dry bones without the Spirit.

The Bible says, "O dry bones, hear the word of the Lord! . . . I will put My Spirit in you, and you shall live . . . Then you shall know that I, the Lord, have spoken it and performed it" (Ezek. 37:4, 14). Also, Pam remarked how much more she received each Thursday at our little meetings, saying they were like the continuation of the Book of Acts. I then shared the reason for not joining her and my excitement at coming across the verse in my Bible reading: "Why do you seek the living among the dead? He is not here, but is risen!" (Luke 24:5–6).

Pam and I joined hands and spirits and prayed while the little ones played. Often she would have the chapter and verse of a psalm come to mind during prayer; this time it was Psalm 32:8. Together we read: "I [the Lord] will instruct you and teach you in the way you should go; I will counsel you with My eye upon you" (AMP). We both remarked that that was one we needed to learn. I reached for a pen and noticing writing on it, I began to read: "I [the Lord] will instruct you and teach you in the way you should go; I will counsel you with My eye upon you" (Ps. 32:8, AMP). (I still have that pen.) We had a great time of rejoicing over the very unusual confirmation on hearing such a profound word from our Teacher.

One lady who attended our group had recently joined the Catholic Church and seldom missed a Love and Praise meeting. She was having a difficult time with childlike simplicity and was having trouble reading and believing Scripture. One day, out of sheer frustration, she remarked how previously, when she was involved in Gurdjieff (a cult that stresses self-knowledge), she would sit and meditate for hours, but couldn't read the Bible for fifteen minutes. (Later someone commented to me privately, she obviously didn't have to fight the world, the flesh, and the devil to meditate.) She frequently expounded on her search for a higher consciousness and her quest for wisdom. We tried to explain that "the fear of the Lord is the beginning of knowledge" and a trusting childlike heart is all the Lord requires (Prov. 1:7). This seemed to escape her as she continued to read and study various intellectual books. She often remarked she wasn't sure where the author was coming from and confessed to becoming more confused by the minute.

> Trust in the LORD with all your heart, and lean not on your own understanding; in all your ways acknowledge Him, and He shall direct your paths.
> —PROVERBS 3:5–6

When her husband became ill, she asked me and another lady from our group to go to the hospital and pray for him. He appeared to have had a wonderful encounter with the one true God; this greatly pleased her after his lifelong profession of being an agnostic. A short time later he died. Instead of being grateful for his turning to the Lord, she became very angry at God for allowing his death, saying she wanted another forty-four years of marriage. We all tried to get her to focus on God's many blessings; one day she stopped at our home to drop off an armload of Christian books and her Bible, stating prayer didn't work. It was heartbreaking to listen to her say she no longer wanted to hear about the things of God. I remember the pain and sadness I felt as she drove away full of such bitterness. I begged God for enlightenment as to what had happened. His answer seemed to come with the thought that she had at one time been involved in falsehood and never completely renounced it; now she had chosen to return to it. She later died of Alzheimer's. We trust in God's mercy for her to have had a change of heart toward His Word.

> If you confess with your mouth the Lord Jesus and believe in your heart that God has raised Him from the dead, you will be saved. For with the heart one believes unto righteousness, and with the mouth confession is made unto salvation. For the Scripture says, "Whoever believes on Him will not be put to shame." . . . For "whoever calls on the name of the Lord shall be saved."
> —Romans 10: 9–13

Midge, one of the original four that began the Love and Praise Prayer Group, was a favorite of everyone. She had a gentle, loving spirit that drew others to the Jesus in her. She never married, but had a great love for children. She won the hearts of our little boys with her many treats and especially when she would go out in the yard to pet their dog, Tippy. Midge was invited to attend our boys' first communions and was included in family celebrations. Even after the prayer meeting moved, we kept in touch. One day I couldn't cease praying for Midge and felt an urgency to visit her; I was saddened to see how this beautiful lady had failed. She had been having trouble with her eyesight and asked if I would help pay her bills. In a short period of time, she could no longer see to drive or even read. With the help of an agency, I was able to get live-in help for her, which worked well until the help moved away. By then, she needed constant care; it was a great challenge to find a place that would take a blind lady and her little dog, Sweetie Pie. After much prayer, a home became available not far from where we lived. Midge had one brother who resided in another part of the state and she was devastated when he passed away. Her two nephews seldom came to visit. My heart ached to see how lonely this precious lady was. She spent most of her time sitting alone, holding and talking to her little dog; a smile would appear on her dear face as I read from her favorite book, the Bible. My daughter-in-law would visit with my two little grand-daughters. They delighted Midge with their hugs and their singing. After eight years of great suffering, God took her to be with Him in Paradise.

> And the ransomed of the LORD shall return, and come to Zion with singing, with everlasting joy on their heads. They shall obtain joy and gladness, and sorrow and sighing shall flee away.
>
> —ISAIAH 35:10

Mary came from the east to spend the winters with her daughter and family; she was thrilled to hear about our prayer group and seldom missed a meeting. She was diagnosed with a bad heart that required surgery. Later, when praying for her, I had the thought that she, like Hezekiah, would be given fifteen more years. I never shared that with her, but did share it with the ladies praying for her. Years later, she needed a ride home from an Aglow meeting. I asked her how long it had been since her heart surgery and she said it had been fourteen years. She went to heaven the following year.

> I have heard your prayer, I have seen your tears; surely I will add to your days fifteen years.
>
> —ISAIAH 38:5

We learned many new and wonderful teachings from God's Holy Word at each meeting. We were discovering in the psalms how good it is to praise God. From reading, "Let everything that has breath praise the Lord," we were each making a concerted effort to praise and thank Him in and for all things (Ps. 150:6). The ongoing blessings, as a result, were nothing short of amazing. Putting the Word to work really did work!

There was special concern, however, for one who continued to complain about everything, in spite of her numerous blessings. I was able to share with her how grumbling kept the Israelites in the desert for forty years, and jokingly said I would not look forward to another "lap around the desert." She wanted me to call and remind her each week about the meetings, saying she got so much out of them. It was frustrating dealing with her due to her lack of commitment. While praying for her, I had a mental picture of the Prayer Group on a large, well-lit, open boat, merrily floating along on a body of water. Suddenly, there were shouts from the shore. Looking back, we discovered it was this lady, but no one was able to turn the boat around to go back for her.

A few days later I was at the store filling a bag of oranges and I heard a friendly hello. I turned to greet this same woman. My greeting was followed by her usual grumbling as to why she had missed another meeting and her ongoing complaints. Her next statement almost took my breath away; I nearly dropped the oranges. She said, "Sometimes I feel like I'm just missing the boat." All I could do was hug her with the love of the Lord and wonder how God puts up with any of us.

> A merry heart does good, like medicine, but a broken spirit dries the bones.
>
> —Proverbs 17:22

A longtime acquaintance called for prayer for her family. The list was very lengthy and after praying for all her needs, I suggested that we intercede for some of our friends who had also called for prayer. She said she didn't have time to be bothered with other people's problems as she had enough of her own.

Sadly, I was reminded of a joke I'd heard, about a lady whose constant prayer was, "Please, Lord, bless my husband and me, our son and daughter; just us four and no more." I definitely prefer to pray God's way:

> Bear one another's burdens, and so fulfill the law of Christ.
>
> —Galatians 6:2

Several years after the Love and Praise Group began I was talking with a lady who attended the meetings when her job permitted. She said when she drove by our street and saw our white house it reminded her of a lighthouse, there to rescue many people in need of prayer. Instantly, the mental picture I had received when coming home from the hospital after surgery came to mind. At the base of a granite mountain an archway had appeared. Looking through it I could see calm water with sailboats going toward a lighthouse in the distance. Due to the awesome peace and presence of the Lord, there was an assurance in my spirit that someday this would make sense. Now it did! Because of one more child, surgery, and my no longer being able to attend the Monday night prayer meeting, the good Lord had made a way for the Love and Praise Prayer Group to come into existence.

> And we know that all things work together for good to those who love God, to those who are the called according to His purpose.
>
> —ROMANS 8:28

A very interesting experience happened when Lisa, who was healed of smoking after a Love and Praise meeting, and I were asked to go to a hospital to pray for a dear, elderly lady who often attended our meetings with her daughter. We always went to pray in twos, as the Bible states that Jesus "began to send them out two by two" (Mark 6:7). After praying and reading several Bible verses, the lady in the next bed pulled back her curtain and asked if we would also pray for her. Lisa had had a strong feeling we should pray for her even before she asked. She was a beautiful black lady who told us she had been "tarrying for the Holy Spirit baptism" for thirty years. We began to share that all she had to do was ask Jesus to baptize her with His Spirit and He would, because "whatever things you ask in prayer, believing, you will receive" (Matt. 21:22). It was so simple she had missed it, thinking she wasn't ready. After a short prayer she began to pray in her heavenly language. This went on for hours, according to our elderly friend. The next day she had a heart transplant which didn't take. She then went to be with Jesus, no doubt praising Him all the way.

> And when Paul had laid hands on them, the Holy Spirit came upon them, and they spoke with tongues...
>
> —ACTS 19:6

Ruth called, asking if she could bring Dee over for prayer for the Holy Spirit baptism. Of course, that was and still is one of our favorite things to do. We spent time teaching Dee the need for repentance and renouncing sin, especially sins against the first commandment by serving false gods. We then stressed the need to make Jesus the Lord of her life. Seldom had we seen anyone so hungry for knowledge of the true God. With a simple and sincere prayer, she asked Jesus to forgive every sin, to come into her heart as her Lord and Savior, and to baptize her with His Holy Spirit. Earlier, when talking about false gods, I had suggested that it was a good idea to clean her house of every trace of evil, as some things can actually act as a magnet for the evil one. Satan feels welcome among filthy books, magazines, videos, anything of the occult, etc. This dear woman went home and gathered all the things she could find pertaining to the occult, false religions, and evil of any kind, and burned them in the fireplace. The next day she told how the fire had become so hot, it cracked her new fireplace. The ouija board nearly scared her to death as it jumped around screeching and trying to get out of the fireplace screen, before it finally burned. Empowered by the Holy Spirit, Dee was committed to following Jesus with her whole heart.

> And you will seek Me and find Me, when you search for Me with all your heart.
>
> —JEREMIAH 29:13

Before long, Dee's car was covered with Christian stickers; she even painted *Hallelujah* on her roof so pilots could also praise God. In spite of others teasing her, she had taken a mighty stand for the Lord of her life. I was full of encouragement, reminding her that at least she was a fan of the God of the universe, and not merely fanatic over a team throwing around a pigskin ball. She fed on God's Word day and night and was experiencing firsthand that "man shall not live by bread alone, but by every word that proceeds from the mouth of God" (Matt. 4:4).

On the other hand, one lady came to Love and Praise who appeared to have no interest in Scripture. She had the trials of Job. Regardless of other prayer requests, none were comparable to hers. Often she was prayed for and encouraged to read God's Word, where the rest of us were finding answers and solutions to our trials. A major change was taking place in most of our lives as we studied and applied the Word of God, especially when we learned that "death and life are in the power of the tongue, and those who love it will eat its fruit" (Prov. 18:21). However, due to focusing entirely on her problems, she just couldn't hear.

I felt such compassion for the many sufferings of this family, and yet I was frustrated at the lack of answered prayer for them. I begged God to show me why this was so. My immediate thought was to read John 15:7, which states, "If you abide in Me, and My words abide in you, you will ask what you desire, and it shall be done for you." As I meditated on this, I could not recall her ever bringing a Bible or showing any interest in reading it. She acted as though it was Protestant and preferred to stay with her rituals. Mark 7:8 states: "For laying aside the commandment of God, you hold the tradition of men." I tried to share the healing and power available through God's Word, but to no avail. After many years of listening and praying, I finally gave up trying to help someone who appeared to reject the healing of His Word. The Bible states that "He sent His Word and healed them, and delivered them from their destructions" (Ps 107:20). I was also reminded of Jesus asking the man at the pool of Bethesda, "Do you want to be made well?" (John 5:6).

Kay, who only occasionally attended the meetings, had been crippled for many years and walked with a cane. One day, when in great pain, she called for prayer. During prayer, I had a mental picture of her jumping rope, so I hesitatingly shared it with her. She began to cry and said she actually had a jump rope under her sink; two of her greatest desires were to jump rope and ride a bicycle again. The Lord is "acquainted with all my ways. For there is not a word on my tongue, But behold, O Lord, You know it altogether" (Ps. 139:3–4). Kay was quite elderly and never jumped rope or rode a bike again, but we read in God's Word to "delight yourself also in the Lord, And He shall give you the desires of your heart" (Ps. 37:4). Hopefully, she is now enjoying both of these activities in heaven.

One of the biggest challenges of the entire group was a little lady who had gone through a divorce and was consumed with anger and bitterness. Hour after hour she studied God's Word, listened to tapes, and attended every Bible teaching she could find. Her spiritual growth, however, could only go so far due to the hatred in her heart. We studied numerous scriptures on forgiveness, but still her heart remained hardened. The Bible says, "Therefore, as the Holy Spirit says: 'Today, if you will hear His voice, Do not harden your hearts...'" (Heb. 3:7–8).

She frequently phoned two or three times a day, usually in tears. One day, she called to inform me that she was going on a fast and did not intend to leave her apartment until God brought her husband back. Several in the group took food and prayed with her, but there was growing concern for her welfare. I sought the Lord for a breakthrough, since she would listen to no one. During prayer, the thought came that she was testing

God and by so doing would miss any blessing He had for her. The next day, I went to visit and shared this. It was wonderful to see her reaction. The hatred in her eyes disappeared, as amid copious tears, she repented of testing God.

> "Be angry, and do not sin": do not let the sun go down on your wrath, nor give place to the devil.
> —Ephesians 4:26–27

This all reminded me of the saying: "Bitterness is like acid; it destroys the vessel in which it is stored, rather than the one on whom you wish it poured." After many healings, this dear sister went to be with the Lord where she received her complete healing.

Several women in our group later confessed to thoughts of divorce. They each had a change of heart, after learning from God's Word that He hates divorce. The Bible says, "For the Lord God of Israel says that He hates divorce" (Mal. 2:16). One lady's husband had left her for another woman, but he begged to come back. She called, asking what she should do. We prayed over the phone seeking God's wisdom for "when you make a vow to God, do not delay to pay it... Better not to vow than to vow and not pay" (Eccles. 5:4–5). Because she still loved him and had the grace of God to forgive, he did move home and they had many more happy years together, before he passed away.

> Blessed are the merciful, for they shall obtain mercy.
> —Matthew 5:7

I felt impressed during one meeting to ask people to memorize Psalm 23. A few weeks later, Nellie's son was diagnosed with a brain tumor. The prayer chain was activated immediately. Thank God, he survived and is doing well today. His dear mother told of memorizing the 23rd Psalm and repeating it, again and again, as she sat by his bed; nothing comforted her like the precious Word of God. Today, Nellie and her husband, Tim, are mighty intercessors for the body of Christ, using the sword of the Word.

> For the word of God is living and powerful, and sharper than any two-edged sword...and is a discerner of the thoughts and intents of the heart.
>
> —HEBREWS 4:12

Later, I read the book *Terror at Tenerife,* in which the author, Norman Williams, describes his miraculous escape from one of the worst airline disasters in history.[1] During the ordeal he kept repeating: "I stand upon Your Word. I stand upon Your Word."

> Heaven and earth will pass away, but My words will by no means pass away.
>
> —MATTHEW 24:35

The son of one of our members was in a small plane crash. Immediately upon receiving the news, his mother began to pray in the Spirit as she drove to the hospital. Her son was not seriously injured; however, the pilot of the small plane that hit his plane was killed. More and more, we were learning to lean on the mercy and truth of God's Word, trusting in Him for His protection.

> For He shall give His angels charge over you, to keep you in all your ways. In their hands they shall bear you up, lest you dash your foot against a stone.
>
> —PSALM 91:11–12

A well-known Dominican priest was to speak in a nearby city, and I was asked to fill a bus with those planning to attend. My telephone rang from seven in the morning until ten at night; exasperated, I called out to God. The thought came that He, too, was frustrated at the great lengths many go to, to hear someone talk about Him, when they could meet Him personally every day. I was impressed, during prayer, with the thought that He shared His glory with no one, and would make sure there would be time to focus on Him. The evening of the big event, the emcee informed the packed crowd there would be a delay due to the speaker's plane being fogged in, in the southern part of the state. There was indeed ample time to praise the Lord of lords and King of kings, just as He had impressed me earlier. The priest taught on the need to be filled with God's Holy Spirit. He stressed that the operation of the gifts from 1 Corinthians 12 should be the norm in every Christian home.

Oscar was most enthused to hear a Dominican priest give such a powerful teaching from God's Word. He had attended a Dominican high school and had great respect for the Order of Preachers. Afterward, coming home from the meeting on the bus, Oscar and I were discussing the priest's teaching about the need for every Christian to operate in the gifts of the Holy Spirit. Oscar remarked how blessed our family was to be experiencing these marvelous gifts. I told him about our youngest son often getting the blessed oil and asking me to come pray over the dog. Soon after prayer, the arthritis seemed to subside, and Tippy would once again run around the yard. We jokingly wondered if praying over the family dog to be healed would ever become the norm.

It was getting later and later one Thursday afternoon and no one had come to the meeting. I checked to see if I had the wrong day and then decided it would be a twosome of the Lord and me. After a time of praising Him, I opened to: "And whoever gives one of these little ones only a cup of cold water... shall by no means lose his reward" (Matt. 10:42). I felt the satisfaction of being blessed because I had obeyed and prepared for the meeting, whether anyone came or not. Just then, the women began to come and we had another wonderful meeting. In spite of people running late, I had enjoyed a sweet lesson from my Master.

A painful lesson was learned when a woman began attending Love and Praise with an agenda. It was obvious she wanted to take charge with her lengthy stories and prayers. One day, she began to sing and continued singing song after song without a break. Hearing that the baby was awake, I went back to get him up from his nap. After changing him, I got on my knees begging the Lord for wisdom as to how to handle this person. Desperate for an answer, I quickly opened a Bible and began to read: "I hear that there are divisions among you, and in part I believe it. For there must also be factions among you, that those who are approved may be recognized among you" (1 Cor. 11:18–19). Momentarily, I pondered the awesomeness of my Teacher and then went back to the meeting with His fresh insight. In spite of this situation becoming such an annoyance, all I seemed to sense was to be patient and love her.

The following week, Gina, one of the pillars of the group, came early; she felt led to sit next to me where the one causing a disturbance usually tried to sit. Others began to recognize the problem and also started to intercede for the Lord's wisdom regarding it; soon that person decided to leave the Love and Praise Group. Several days later, my husband brought in the mail; after quietly reading something he let out a groan. Attempting to protect me, he had opened and read a letter from that lady. With tear-filled eyes, Oscar said he couldn't believe the hatefulness it contained. He didn't want me to read it, but relented. I was heartbroken to read that she was attributing our beautiful Holy Spirit meetings to the evil one. It was impossible to understand, especially when she knew better. Phone calls came from irate members of the group who had also received the hate-filled letter; it was then that I discovered she had been urging many not to attend the meetings.

I felt, however, that the Lord had previously prepared me for this. A few days earlier, I had had a dream of the group in a large life-raft made of rubber, floating down a beautiful river. We were singing and praising the Lord when someone screamed. Looking back, we could see this lady swimming toward us with a raised dagger in her hand, threatening to tear the raft and sink everyone. I remember being very upset by that dream.

> "No weapon formed against you shall prosper, and every tongue which rises against you in judgment You shall condemn. This is the heritage of the servants of the LORD, and their righteousness is from Me," says the LORD.
>
> —ISAIAH 54:17

My anguished prayer was that our loving heavenly Father would forgive her and, most especially, that she had not done the unforgivable.

> And anyone who speaks a word against the Son of Man, it will be forgiven him; but to him who blasphemes against the Holy Spirit, it will not be forgiven.
>
> —LUKE 12:10

Our Love and Praise Group had been learning about tithing and a true test came when Connie told of the dire needs of another lady that had attended a few times. She needed help to pay her rent so we took up a collection. Oscar had wisely warned me to never collect money for the group, as some might think that was why I had the meetings here. Faith had been appointed for the job. Each person was encouraged to ask the Lord for direction as to what to give. A voice in my head plainly said, "Empty your purse." My first reaction was to flinch; not remembering how much was in it. Out of obedience, I cleaned it out only to find a mere fourteen dollars. That night, I was on my usual high from the meeting. While in bed praising God, the thought came to get up and go look at the check Oscar had just brought home. I went to the kitchen and discovered a bonus check for $1,400; exactly one hundredfold of what I had given by emptying my purse. My childlike faith just grew another notch. It has been said the Lord often judges our hearts by checking our checkbooks.

> Give, and it will be given to you: good measure, pressed down, shaken together, and running over...For with the same measure that you use, it will be measured back to you.
>
> —Luke 6:38

Oscar began winning trips through his work. We enjoyed vacationing in San Diego, Las Vegas, and three consecutive trips to Hawaii. Each time in Hawaii we got together with special friends that had moved there shortly before our first trip. On one visit, when we were out to dinner, my friend, Colleen, remarked she wanted what I had. We went to the ladies lounge where we prayed for her to receive the baptism of the Holy Spirit. Losing all track of time, we were in there for quite a while. Back at our hotel, Oscar asked what took us so long. When I told him about praying with my friend, he was upset saying I shouldn't have forced my beliefs on her and what if I had turned her off to the Lord. I tried to explain she asked for it, but he went to bed disgusted with his fanatical wife. I recall hearing a marvelous Catholic Evangelist admonishing a class never to worry about turning someone off when talking about the Lord, for if they weren't interested, they were already turned off. I sat up to pray, seeking forgiveness if I had missed the Lord on this. While praying, I asked Jesus to please speak to me through His Word. Opening my Bible, I began to read:

> If a son asks for bread from any father among you, will he give him a stone? Or if he asks for a fish, will he give him a serpent instead of a fish? Or if he asks for an egg, will he offer him a scorpion?

Turning the page, I read:

> If you then, being evil, know how to give good gifts to your children, how much more will your heavenly Father give the Holy Spirit to those who ask Him!
> —Luke 11: 11–13

With that, I woke my sleeping husband to explain further, and show him the passage I had just opened to. He apologized, saying he realized how much I tried to do God's will and was finally able to share in my joy over our friend's blessing.

There were also trips to Australia, Athens, Alaska, and Austria. I kidded Oscar about possibly winning trips using all the letters in the alphabet. With grateful hearts, we both recognized the abundant blessings of the Lord, as we strived to walk in His ways.

> Oh, taste and see that the LORD is good; blessed is the man who trusts in Him!
>
> —PSALM 34:8

———

CHAPTER 4

Prayer Group Challenges

———◆◆◆———

A PILLAR OF OUR LOVE AND PRAISE group had been telling her brother-in-law about the meetings. He was a
Jesuit priest who did a lot of counseling, and he asked if he
could attend. The first time he came, this gentle, soft-spoken,
elderly man won all of our hearts. We welcomed him with
open arms. I told him after the meeting that I was uncomfortable seeing a man of the cloth in the back row. He was
emphatic about keeping his back seat and said he was only
there to observe; he began to attend regularly. It wasn't long
before he asked if he could bring some of his clients. I told
him the sign on the door always read: "Welcome, please come
in!" Over the next several weeks, he brought two or three of
the women he was counseling for prayer. He always left with
a warm hug, stating how much he enjoyed the meeting.

One of the ladies, who seldom attended the group,
called to tell me she was shocked that I continued to lead
the meetings with a Jesuit priest present. I told her that I was

also bothered by not having the priest lead the meetings, but that he had insisted he was there to observe. This was the same lady who at a previous meeting was determined that we pray the rosary; great confusion erupted since not everyone was Catholic. Also, the major thrust of a Charismatic prayer meeting was to allow the leading of the Holy Spirit with spontaneous prayer from the heart, which always brought unity. Suddenly, division occurred in our meeting for the first time. Some raised their voices in favor of the rosary while others opposed. One lady got up and walked out, slamming the door as she left. All I could do was send up an SOS to the Holy Spirit. As I prayed, the thought kept coming that this was what happened when we lifted up someone other than Jesus. About that time, the following scripture was read: "But when the Helper comes, whom I shall send to you from the Father, the Spirit of truth who proceeds from the Father, He will testify of Me" (John 15:26). We recognized a great teaching had just occurred. The Holy Spirit, who leads in all truth, was sent to lift up only Jesus.

> And I, if I am lifted up from the earth, will draw all peoples to Myself.
>
> —John 12:32

> A certain woman from the crowd raised her voice and said to Him, "Blessed is the womb that bore You, and the breasts which nursed You!" But He said, "More than that, blessed are those who hear the word of God and keep it!"
>
> —Luke 11:27–28

After further prayer we all realized we needed to heed Mary's only command in the Bible: "His mother said to the servants, 'Whatever He says to you, do it.'" (John 2:5).

Looking back on more than five hundred prayer meetings held in our home, that was the only one to cause disunity; our focus was momentarily off of King Jesus.

Tuesday, of the following week, I received a letter from the Jesuit priest informing me that, from now on, he would be opening the meetings with a twenty minute teaching. I surmised he had been called and asked to take charge by the lady mentioned above, but I never had proof. I had recently learned that he taught classes on hypnosis. He had also studied medicine before becoming a priest and was still very interested in healing. He was even involved in researching the psychic healings taking place in the Philippines. My heart sank! The only instruction I felt the Holy Spirit had given me for facilitating the meetings was to give Him the first half hour in praise and worship and He would take care of the rest of the meeting.

I remember being on the verge of tears, after having just read the letter, when the doorbell rang. There stood Christine, one of the most prayerful members of the group. She had been going by my house and felt compelled to stop. I was so happy to see her and was certain the Lord had directed her footsteps to our door. After a most welcome hug, I showed her the letter. Together, the two of us stormed heaven for an answer. We agreed I had to call the Jesuit priest right away, because he planned to begin his teaching in just two days. With my heart pounding, I dialed his residence, but he was not in. My precious friend remarked that that just gave us more time to pray, which we did. A few minutes later, I called again; this time he answered and was very happy to hear from me. Getting right to the point, I told him I had just received his letter. I added that, as the leader of the Love and Praise Prayer Group, I did not want him to teach; however, he was still welcome to attend. Hearing that, he began to yell so loudly, I held the phone out for Christine to listen. We continued to pray silently while he chastised me for even leading the prayer group. He asked how many degrees I had in theology, and just who I thought I was to be in charge of that meeting, and on and on. Clinging to Christine's hand, I felt the peace of the Lord, and was overcome with love and concern for him. After he paused for a breath, I told him that we all loved him but we were not open to learning about hypnosis. He became very quiet and began to sniffle; after a long pause, he remarked he had never experienced such beautiful faith or seen so much love as he had at those meetings. We said good-bye, and he never attended again.

It was several weeks prior to this episode that Oscar and I had been invited to an eightieth birthday party for Father. We were both very uncomfortable with the people and the conversations. The chief topic was how and when individuals had hypnotized clients. There was also talk of past regression and reincarnation, all of which the Bible condemns. My husband and I were both praying God's protection and left the party as soon as it was polite to do so.

> There shall not be found among you anyone…who conjures spells, or a medium, or a spiritist, or one who calls up the dead. For all who do these things are an abomination to the LORD…
> —DEUTERONOMY 18:10–12

The very next week, I received a two-page letter from our Jesuit, in his beautiful handwriting, stating that God was the Divine Hypnotist and extolling the virtues of hypnotism. Soon the phone began to nearly ring off the wall. Father had sent a copy to all the people that had ever attended the Love and Praise meetings, having taken copies of both the old and new membership lists. There were even calls from former members that had moved to New York and Ohio, asking about a strange letter they had just received.

The following Sunday when I came out of church, my pastor motioned that he wanted to speak with me. He said he had received an unusual letter that week; all I could reply was, "Oh no, not you, too." He began to laugh as I explained and told him the Prayer Group felt hypnosis opened the door to the other side. He mockingly pretended to bite his nails in fear, asking if I really thought there was another side. I said I didn't just think there was another side, I knew there was. Realizing I was not going along with his mockery, he said he had had this priest as a teacher when in the seminary, and thought he was a little squirrelly even then. Later, I received a copy of the political letter my pastor had written in response to the Jesuit. He stated there was obviously a misunderstanding.

On two previous occasions, I had informed my pastor about the prayer meetings held in our home. I extended an invitation to attend since it was in his parish, but he merely walked away both times, giving no response. It was increasingly clear from his homilies that he was not convinced of the truth of God's Word. I remember asking the Holy Spirit, after hearing one of his sermons, why I felt sick inside. The thought came that His Spirit in me was grieved and that I should continue to intercede for my pastor. During prayer for him I randomly opened God's Word and began to read:

> The wise men are ashamed, they are dismayed and taken. Behold, they have rejected the word of the LORD; so what wisdom do they have?
>
> —JEREMIAH 8:9

An elderly nun heard about our meetings and began to attend. She was very scholarly and wanted time to teach. Some in the group were concerned regarding a teaching from her since she never brought a Bible, reminding us of our recent priest episode. By now God's Word was like fresh manna to all of us and nothing else satisfied. We recognized how easily we could get off track without constant teaching from our manual and guidance from the Holy Spirit. We had also learned we were to judge among those calling themselves brothers and sisters, by the fruit of the spirit. This nun, unlike many, appeared haughty and controlling. She seemed to have a hidden agenda and never had time to pray for anyone, which sent up a red flag for all of us. At about her third meeting, she met me at the door and informed me she was "going to teach." Praying in the Spirit, I heard, "She is bringing contamination." I questioned what she had in mind and she said she intended to lead us into an Eastern form of meditation. I reminded her that Psalm 1 stated we were to meditate in God's Word day and night; in my mind that didn't leave room for any other form of meditation (Ps. 1:2). She scoffed at my narrow-mindedness informing me that even the Trappists were open to other forms of meditation, mentioning Thomas Merton. I told her Thomas Merton, known as Father Lewis O.C.S.O., had taught my brother when he, too, was a Trappist monk in Gethsemane, Kentucky. I then commented it had appeared very strange to me that Father Lewis was granted permission, in the first place, to study with the Dalai Lama so as to incorporate his Buddhist ways of meditation. It seemed even stranger that he was not able to bring those teachings back to the dear, holy Christian monks, due to being mysteriously electrocuted while on his visit. According to *Larson's Book of Cults*, by Bob Larson, former Christian missionaries to Tibet reported that, "Tibetan Buddhism is the most openly occultic of all non-Christian world religions. Even the monks themselves make no pretense about their consorting with demonic demigods."[1]

> I am the LORD your God...You shall have no other gods before Me.
> —EXODUS 20:2–3

> For You have forsaken Your people, the house of Jacob, because they are filled with eastern ways.
> —ISAIAH 2:6

> They served their idols, which became a snare to them.
> —PSALM 106:36

When this sister realized she wasn't going to teach her form of meditation, she left in a huff, not even speaking to the lady coming up the walk.

These were two of the most difficult encounters during those years. Growing up in a very Catholic home and attending Catholic schools where I had been taught great respect for all clergy, I had done the unthinkable by taking a stand against them. However, there was peace in my heart knowing I had stayed true to God's Word.

> As we have said before, so now I say again, if anyone preaches any other gospel to you than what you have received, let him be accursed. For do I now persuade men, or God? Or do I seek to please men? For if I still pleased men, I would not be a bondservant of Christ.
> —GALATIANS 1:9–10

CHAPTER 5

Godly Ancestry

—■◆■—

T HERE HAD BEEN AN UNUSUAL NUMBER of serious prayer requests at a particular Love and Praise meeting. Afterward, one lady questioned me about the blessings my family walked in, intimating that we were due for some problems. This comment brought fear to my heart which I knew I must deal with.

> For God has not given us a spirit of fear, but of power and of love and of a sound mind.
>
> —2 TIMOTHY 1:7

That evening, I got on my knees and inquired of the Lord as to why we did seem to be very blessed. As I prayed in the Spirit, the thought clearly came, "Praise and thank Me for your Godly ancestry." Asking the Lord to speak through His Word, I opened *The New American Bible* and began to read: "Now will I praise those godly men, our ancestors, each in his own time" (Sirach 44:1). Once again, a confirmation had come through randomly opening the blessed Living Word. I began to ponder the truth that had just been revealed.

Both of my parents had come from generations of God-fearing, strict, Irish Catholic backgrounds; each was the youngest of nine siblings. My father could trace his roots to Charles Carroll; the only Catholic and last surviving signer of the Declaration of Independence, and to John Carroll; the first Catholic Bishop in the United States and founder of Georgetown University. Cardinal Gibbons, the second American to be named a cardinal, was also in the bloodline.

Dad's immediate family was remarkable. His oldest brother was a Trappist monk for over fifty years, both of his sisters were Mercy nuns in the nursing profession, and child number eight was a Franciscan priest, ordained in Rome. My dad had recalled how his father read the Bible every night, along with a book on the lives of the saints.

When I read Psalms 1:2–3: "But his delight is in the law of the LORD, and in His law he meditates day and night....whatever he does shall prosper," I recognize the truth of God's Word in my grandfather's life. As a young man he came to America from Ireland, following his father's death. Working his way across the states, he homesteaded in Iowa where he met and married my grandmother. They were blessed with nine children. He died before I was born, but stories were told of what a prayerful man he was. My mother's family would see him walking many miles, through snow and ice, to attend a mission. Everything he touched turned to gold. If he raised cattle, the price went up just as he sold them; the same thing happened with sheep, his crops, or whatever he tried.

Blessed shall be the fruit of your body, the produce of
your ground and the increase of your herds...
—DEUTERONOMY 28:4

He owned the first tractor west of the Mississippi and
kept his seven sons busy by purchasing land to farm. He
became one of the wealthiest men in the county. Troubled
that his worldly goods were becoming idols and fearful of
serving mammon more than his God, he gave everything
to his wife and children. With my grandmother's permission, he entered a Trappist monastery, joining his oldest son,
Brother Jerome.

No servant can serve two masters; for either he will hate
the one and love the other, or else he will be loyal to the
one and despise the other. You cannot serve God and
mammon.
—LUKE 16:13

His life at the monastery consisted of prayer, silence,
fasting, and work, which continued to bless the monastery.
He died in his sixties. Shortly after his death, my dad entered
the same Trappist monastery where he took his father's reli-
gious name of Brother James. Due to the severe fasting and
the difficult lifestyle, he left after six months, for which I am
very grateful.

My father was the most prayerful man I have ever known.
The family rosary, litanies, and numerous prayers were said at
our home every evening. Dad would usually still be kneeling in prayer as I lovingly kissed him on the forehead, before
going to bed. Often in the morning he would be in the same
spot, at the end of the kitchen table, deep in prayer before
starting his day. This scripture comes to mind:

Train up a child in the way he should go, and when he is old he will not depart from it.

—Proverbs 22:6

His father had certainly been a good teacher! On Sunday afternoons dad would get out the Baltimore Catechism for a quiz on what Mother had taught us after Mass in her Catechism Class. On Sunday evenings in the winter, Mother would make fudge and popcorn for us to enjoy as we played family games. The Sabbath was a day of church, rest, and growing closer to the Lord and each other; it was always my favorite day of the week.

Mother also had beautiful faith; trusting God was a way of life, having been taught this from her godly parents. When a bad storm arose, she would light the blessed candle symbolizing the light of Christ. We would gather on our knees praying the rosary and asking God's protection. In thirty-six years of farming the family farm, only once did we experience a crop failure. The hail stones and destructive wind seemed to stop at our fence lines. A couple of neighbors asked my dad what kind of prayers we said at our house. I doubt if he responded as to how faith-filled those prayers were.

Therefore I say to you, whatever things you ask when you pray, believe that you receive them, and you will have them.

—Mark 11:24

In the country the splendor of God's world was evident everywhere, from the first brilliant rays at sunrise, causing the dew-filled grass to sparkle like a field of diamonds, to the fading pink and purple clouds, as the crimson sun sank beneath the horizon. The night air could be fresh and crisp, or warm and humid. We frequently marveled at the magnificent full moon or at the clear, star-filled sky glistening overhead. Mother would point out the Milky Way, the Big and Little Dippers, and various constellations as we kids gazed into the heavens.

> When I consider Your heavens, the work of Your fingers, the moon and the stars, which You have ordained, what is man that You are mindful of him, and the son of man that You visit him?
> —PSALM 8:3–4

Often, there would be a shout from a member of the family to come outside and enjoy the beauty of a double rainbow. Its brilliance overpowered the dark clouds and reminded us of God's covenant.

> I set My rainbow in the cloud, and it shall be for the sign of the covenant between Me and the earth.
> —GENESIS 9:13

There was excitement at seeing the first robin redbreast after a long, cold winter and realizing the warmth of spring was on its way. Newborn kittens, calves, and freshly hatched chicks were all wonders of the Almighty's creation.

> For since the creation of the world His invisible attributes are clearly seen…
> —ROMANS 1:20

Most of the many animals we had were named and given the best possible care. When working in the field, Dad would get down from the tractor and carefully pick up a bird's nest that was on the ground before him. He would walk a great distance to gently place it safely outside the fence. He was rewarded later by the beautiful song of the meadowlark. There was always a wonderful love and respect fostered for all of our heavenly Father's creations.

> If a bird's nest happens to be before you along the way, in any tree or on the ground, with young ones or eggs...you shall surely let the mother go...that it may be well with you and that you may prolong your days.
> —Deuteronomy 22:6

My older brother, at age eight or nine, had a pet hen named Winnie. In the fall, when most of the chickens were to be sold, Winnie was secretly stowed in a separate shed. The following morning, when my brother went to set her free, he found a stiff little hen, due to the sudden drop in temperature during the night. In tears, he decided to have a funeral for her. He loved to play priest and say Mass; he got fully vested using lace curtains and other materials from Mother's sewing room. Winnie was laid out in a shoe box lined with satin, also from the sewing room. My younger brother wheeled the casket down the aisle of the pretend church in the grove, using his outgrown stroller. I was the chief musician striking a bucket with two sticks and singing a mournful tune. The sermon was great and the three of us were pleased at the wonderful service. My older brother was so enthused he lined up two more funerals. By the third service, I had had it and began to sing the then popular song, "Pistol Packin' Momma." This brought shouts that I was ruining the Mass and the chase was on; due to his long vestments, I outran him into the safety of Mother's arms. She wisely suggested he finish the service without "the choir."

Life was beautifully sweet, simple, and secure. My father

was there for every meal and to pray with us every night. Mother took great delight in pleasing her family with what an uncle termed "a banquet at every meal." Dad was treated like a king and Mother was his queen. She set a great example for me by daily preparing good meals and keeping an immaculate house for her family and not just when guests came. I was always impressed to see her run the comb through her hair, add fresh lipstick, and grab a clean apron when she heard dad's tractor coming in from the field. No wonder we had such a pleasant home; Dad was the head and Mother was the heart. Never did it cross my mind to question my parents' love for each other or for me. Many times my brothers and I have remarked how blessed we were to grow up in such a peaceful and God-fearing home. I loved my childhood. When teased about being a farmer's daughter, I just smile and think to myself, "If you only knew the innumerable blessings."

Our parish priest often preached that parents were obligated to give their children a Catholic education, if they could afford it. Fearful of disobeying the Lord, Dad and Mother sent my brothers and me to Catholic boarding schools for high school and college. This must have been a great sacrifice to have us all leave home at such an early age. I am eternally grateful to them for their selfless love in training me in the way I should go.

> Your ears shall hear a word behind you, saying, "This is the way, walk in it," whenever you turn to the right hand or whenever you turn to the left.
>
> —ISAIAH 30:21

CHAPTER 6

The Holy Spirit Class

ONCE AGAIN, DURING MY PRAYER TIME, an unusual thought kept reoccurring. Over and over in my mind came the words: "It is my desire for you to have a class on the Holy Spirit." I finally decided to run this by my husband, certain he would agree I was much too busy. To my surprise, he thought it was a great idea, stating he felt it was from the Lord. In a state of shock, I asked if he thought I should check with our pastor regarding a place to hold the meetings. Oscar bowed his head, evidently saying a prayer; then he said, "Have it here." Logical man that he was, he wisely suggested Thursday evenings since chairs would already be set up from the afternoon Love and Praise Group. I certainly had not expected his reaction and had difficulty getting to sleep that night; my mind was racing with the many concerns that were filling it. I wondered if this was really from the Lord. Who could help? How would we get the word out? Who would attend? How many books should we order? In a flash, the number thirty came to mind. Releasing the whole thing to my heavenly Father, I finally had a restful sleep.

The following day, I called several from the Love and Praise Group asking for prayer and suggestions. Many were eager to help; one offered name tags leftover from a class at her church saying she thought there were about thirty. I suggested she bring all of them. Interestingly, thirty-three people attended, including a priest, Oscar, and me. I still shudder when I think back to my dry mouth and trembling hands and knees at the start of those meetings.

> I was with you in weakness, in fear, and in much trembling.
>
> —1 CORINTHIANS 2:3

The format for the seven-week class was much like the Love and Praise Meetings, with the exception of having guest speakers. The fifth week, a priest prayed for everyone to receive the baptism of the Holy Spirit. Many lives were changed as a result of those meetings. It is now years later and I still get positive feedback regarding that class on the Holy Spirit.

The desire of my heart has always been to tell others of the wonderful Holy Spirit. I have taught several classes using the book, *The Holy Spirit and You,* by Dennis Bennett, an Episcopal priest.[1] This is an excellent teaching book on the Holy Spirit and His gifts.

Recently, my friend Nellie was here and was reminiscing about the blessings from that Holy Spirit class. It was her husband, Tim, who first noticed the dove shaped stone in our front room fireplace; he had asked if we had it specifically placed there. Oscar and I were both surprised that we had never noticed this obvious shape, but we were blessed nonetheless to see a "dove" flying into our home.

One couple that had attended said their marriage improved as a result of their experience with the Holy Spirit. Another couple's marriage was restored. One man lost the desire to smoke and also of having too much to drink on occasion, thus strengthening his marriage. An older man passed away a few months after attending the class and having met his Savior.

The greatest blessing for Oscar and me was the transformation of a beautiful young girl's life. Her name was Liz. Her neighbor, Janet, attended the Thursday afternoon Love and Praise meetings and encouraged the teenager to come in the evening. After our first greeting and hug, I remember feeling that there was something very special about that tiny little blonde. She had such sadness in her eyes. Even our younger sons asked what was wrong with her. Liz faithfully attended each week with her friend, Janet, and had a great encounter with the Holy Spirit; afterward, when work allowed, she joined the afternoon prayer group. Little by little, we learned the turmoil she was in. Her parents had both died from cancer, her brother lived in the area, and her older sister resided in another part of the state. Liz had befriended a young man on the bus by offering the bus fare he lacked. He later had moved in with her and she was expecting his child.

The prayer group had a baby shower, and Tammy, that gorgeous baby girl, became the pet of our group. My family considered this special little mother and baby as relatives. Oscar tried to find work for the father; however, the young man got into drugs which caused Liz and baby to leave him. In a rage, he burned the apartment down. Thank God, no one was injured, but the treasures from her deceased parents were destroyed along with all the baby gifts. She lived with her brother until she found another apartment. One day Liz called sobbing as she told me the baby was in the hospital with pneumonia. Tammy had caught a cold, riding on the back of her bicycle, as Liz took her to daycare in the rain. Our oldest son came from work just as I had hung up the phone and was still in tears. Hearing the situation, he went to his room and soon came out with a large check, requesting we purchase a car for Liz. He had one condition: that we not say where the money came from. I told him God would surely bless him for his generosity in doing such a good deed.

Liz and little Tammy were God's gifts to our lives. Often Liz and I would get together for prayer. The following mental picture occurred regularly as the two of us prayed: this darling young woman was climbing the side of a mountain wearing large army boots. The climb was so steep, rocky, and difficult that her toes were bleeding as they protruded from the boots. Below, to the right of the cliff, was a straight, well-lit path, which reminded me of the yellow brick road in the movie *The Wizard of Oz*. The following verse would come to mind:

> For I know the thoughts that I think toward you, says the LORD, thoughts of peace and not of evil, to give you a future and a hope.
>
> —JEREMIAH 29:11

Many nights I tossed and turned praying for direction and wisdom for Liz and the baby. All I could do was trust that somehow God would direct her footsteps to that straight, well-lit path He so frequently showed me. The Holy Spirit's comfort was continually available through His Word.

> Fear not, for I am with you; be not dismayed, for I am your God. I will strengthen you, yes, I will help you, I

will uphold you with My righteous right hand.

—ISAIAH 41:10

Liz had a great hunger for the things of God. After purchasing a car she liked, she soon was able to attend a church where she met Tom, a godly young man. Later they were married, honeymooned in Hawaii, and by the end of their first year were expecting a baby. They were at our home for dinner when contractions started, so off to the hospital they went; Tammy, now almost four, stayed with us. The excitement was building since this was the first birth our younger boys had been exposed to. Around midnight the distressed father called in tears stating they had lost the baby. My husband and I, in a state of shock and disbelief, got dressed and headed for the hospital where we discovered there was no longer a heartbeat for the baby. Our precious Liz labored the rest of the night only to give birth to a beautiful, lifeless baby boy. The pain and suffering were almost unbearable.

Oscar had noticed the name tag on the labor and delivery nurse and recognized the family name as belonging to our parish. This sweet, young woman with beautiful, blue eyes, impressed both of us with her professionalism and her loving care and compassion. When driving home from the hospital, we both commented on what a lovely girl she was. Oscar stunned me by saying somehow he felt she was to be our daughter-in-law; I was simply amazed because I had had the same feeling. I remember saying, "Honey, let's pray this might be the one."

In the morning, when the boys came for breakfast, we shared the sad news. Each reaction was one of questioning why so much tragedy happened to this sweet little woman. Oscar was eager to share about the lovely nurse with our oldest son who had just broken up with his girlfriend. Our son had known the nurse and her family for many years. His face lit up, recalling how beautiful he had always thought she was, and he, too, remarked about her lovely eyes. I was reminded of the following verse: "The lamp of the body is the eye. Therefore, when your eye is good, your whole body is also full of light" (Luke 11:34). I promised to get the up-to-date information about her love life.

Soon, the weary father came for breakfast; his eyes were swollen from tears and grief. The toddler came running asking about Mommy and wanting to see *her* baby. Tom took Tammy on his knee and told her God had taken their baby to heaven. She said, "Oh," jumped down and ran back to her cartoons. Shortly, she returned asking, "Why?" The Lord must have been pleased at the patient and loving way this father handled such a difficult situation. I was very impressed and couldn't stop thanking God, as I witnessed His answer to our many prayers. He had provided the perfect husband and father for our precious little friend and her child, wonderfully fulfilling His Word.

> For I know the thoughts that I think toward you, says the LORD, thoughts of peace and not of evil, to give you a future and a hope.
>
> —JEREMIAH 29:11

As a distraction, I asked Tom about the darling nurse. During the long night the young couple had asked if she was married. They discovered she was very much single, having just broken up with her boyfriend. This was music to my ears; I could hardly wait to share the good news with Oscar and our son.

The following Sunday, the two singles met at Mass. Our son made a point of talking to the cute nurse to ask about our little friend, Liz. Once she realized Oscar and I were his parents, she said the nurses had been advised to take pictures of the stillborn babies as it helped the parents with their grieving process; she had taken a picture of the beautiful baby boy and needed the young couple's address. Needless to say, our son got her phone number promising to call soon with the desired address. This was the beginning of a beautiful courtship leading to a wonderful marriage that has blessed us with two gorgeous granddaughters.

> Call to Me, and I will answer you, and show you great and mighty things, which you do not know.
> —JEREMIAH 33:3

I recall when praying about the right girl for our oldest son to marry, the thought always came that she was "right under our nose." His bride grew up less than a mile from where we lived, attended the same church, grammar and high schools, and even had the same zip code. Her sister was in his class. In the eighth grade he had attended a swim party at her house, but didn't pay attention to the then fifth-grader. One of the greatest blessings for us was discovering our new daughter-in-law had obeyed her parents by breaking up with a young man they didn't think was right for her. Our son had also obeyed us in breaking up with his last girlfriend for the same reason. God always blesses obedience!

I remember telling our son God would surely bless him for his act of kindness in giving our little friend, Liz, money to buy a car. That car was used to get her to church, where she met and married Tom, a wonderful, godly man. The following year, at the birth of their baby, Oscar and I met the lovely nurse from the labor and delivery ward. When our single son discovered the nurse was also single, they began to date; she later became the wife our son and all of us had been praying for. Once again, we are enjoying the many blessings of obedience. We can never outgive our heavenly Father.

> Give, and it will be given to you: good measure, pressed down, shaken together, and running over will be put into your bosom. For with the same measure that you use, it will be measured back to you.
>
> —Luke 6:38

As a postscript, Liz has often remarked about the unconditional love she felt at that Holy Spirit class. Because she didn't feel condemned or judged, she was eager to know the Jesus being presented. I know of few people that have suffered more than this little saint. She lost both parents to cancer when she was very young, had a child out of wedlock, her boyfriend burned their apartment containing all the priceless treasures from her deceased parents, and she experienced poverty as a single parent. After her marriage, their first home was flooded, she delivered a stillborn son, and in the last several years her sister, and then her brother died at young ages. Through it all, Liz has clung to Jesus, the Lord of her life; what a prayer warrior she has become! She has been tested through the fire and is coming out as pure gold.

> …you have been grieved by various trials, that the genuineness of your faith, being much more precious than gold that perishes, though it is tested by fire, may be found to praise, honor, and glory at the revelation of Jesus Christ, whom having not seen you love.
>
> —1 Peter 1:6–8

She and her husband have been blessed with two more beautiful children. Their lovely family walks very close to the Lord and enjoys His many blessings. Glory to God!

> I sought the LORD, and He heard me, and delivered me from all my fears.... Oh, taste and see that the LORD is good; blessed is the man who trusts in Him!
>
> —PSALM 34:4, 8

CHAPTER 7

Mary Bernadette

———◆———

OSCAR AND I WERE MARRIED FEBRUARY 11, 1956, on the feast of Our Lady of Lourdes. Like most good Catholics, we both had great devotion to the Blessed Mother. Years earlier, I had seen the movie *Song of Bernadette* and fell in love with the saint and the name. When expecting our second child, I remember hoping for a girl since we had already been blessed with a darling son. We were thrilled to welcome a beautiful little girl into our young family and christen her, Mary Bernadette.

> Behold, children are a heritage from the LORD, the fruit
> of the womb is a reward.
>
> —PSALM 127:3

We had purchased our first house just before our son was born. I loved being a stay-at-home mom and able to put into practice all the homemaking skills learned from my wonderful mother. Oscar frequently expressed his appreciation over the good meals, clean house, and our "great kids." He loved to play with the children, realizing how much he had missed in not having had a brother or sister. Life was absolutely wonderful!

Shortly before Mary's second birthday, dear friends had invited us for dinner. Mary spent time playing with their little boy; no one realized he was coming down with the flu. The next day, my friend, Ileane, called to see if our children were OK since their baby was very sick with the flu. A day or two later, Mary began to throw up and then started with diarrhea. I called our pediatrician who informed me there was a flu epidemic. He asked me not to bring her into the office full of sick children, saying he would stop to check her on his way home from work.

After the doctor arrived and examined Mary, he immediately went to the phone to call the hospital. He raised his voice, sternly requesting she be put in the hall if necessary, stating she was beginning to dehydrate. He left, saying he would grab a bite to eat and meet us at the hospital. Fortunately, my younger brother was living with us at the time and stayed with our three-year-old son while Oscar and I rushed the baby to Emergency. The wait seemed like an eternity! Finally, there was an available bed in a room with three other babies, one of whom was in an oxygen tent due to pneumonia. After begging a harried nurse for some care, we were informed that our child was the twenty-first baby to be brought in to the large Chicago hospital that evening, and would be dealt with accordingly. Suddenly, we noticed Mary had gone into a blank stare and wasn't responding. In a panic, Oscar grabbed an intern to come and look at our baby. He told us she had gone into a coma, as he ran to get help. Several doctors came into the small room and asked us to leave. We headed for the chapel; together, we begged God to heal our precious little girl. Later, Oscar told me he had lit a candle and saw it go out; he was praying that wasn't a sign that her light on this earth would also be extinguished. Early the next morning, our darling little Mary Bernadette went to the loving arms of her Maker; she had contracted pneumonia.

> But Jesus said, "Let the little children come to Me, and do not forbid them; for of such is the kingdom of heaven."
>
> —MATTHEW 19:14

We had experienced the sting of death for the first time six months earlier. Oscar's parents were vacationing in Italy for the summer when his father died of a sudden heart attack. That was still an open wound, but this was agonizing pain like we had never imagined. We clung to each other crying as though our hearts would break. How could we explain this to our three-year-old? Oh, how we thanked God for him.

At Mary Bernadette's wake, along with many relatives and friends, numerous others from the large mortuary came to view the "beautiful doll" in the casket. A comforting Mass of the Angels was said at her funeral. She was buried in front of a lovely statue portraying Jesus and the little children. The outpouring of love and support was unforgettable. I will always remember the heartbreak of our friends whose baby was recovering from the flu. Thank God, we continued to be best friends.

The following month, I read in the local paper about a little boy having been run over by a truck. His mother and I had been roommates in the hospital when we had our first babies. I called her immediately. Her husband answered the phone and said Lois wouldn't talk to anyone, for she felt no one understood. She was tired of hearing they could have more children and should thank God for their younger son; she just wanted their Michael back. I then told him about Mary Bernadette; hearing about our heartache, he knew she would talk to me since I would understand. That was the beginning of daily phone calls at lunch time. Lois was having a difficult time dealing with her son's empty chair at the table. We would cry together empathizing with each other's pain as I, too, was looking at an empty chair. The more we shared, the sooner my heart began to heal. I've often come to appreciate the scripture that says, "Give, and it will be given to you... For with the same measure that you use, it will be measured back to you" (Luke 6:38). We still correspond at Christmas; they were blessed with another son and are now also enjoying grandchildren.

The fall of that same year, we drove four hundred miles to attend my younger brother's wedding. Being three months pregnant, I had checked with my doctor regarding the trip; he saw no problem with the drive. The night before the wedding, I began to hemorrhage and was rushed to the hospital where I had a miscarriage. This was a tremendous heartbreak for all of us. There had been such great anticipation and happiness over the prospect of another child.

After returning home, I was hospitalized again with hemorrhaging and suffered many years with female problems. A neighbor recommended I make an appointment with her elderly gynecologist; he diagnosed the need for uterine suspension surgery. The doctor advised us to discard our papers for adoption saying he would see me in a year, pregnant with another child. It turned out to be five years before we were blessed with our second son, shortly after our move to the West Coast. It has been said our trials can make us "bitter or better." I pray with Jesus' help ours have been used to make us better and closer to the Holy Spirit, our great Comforter.

> And we know that all things work together for good to those who love God, to those who are called according to His purpose.
>
> —ROMANS 8:28

CHAPTER 8

Blessings of Obedience

———◆———

MANY THINGS BEGAN TO COME INTO focus as I meditated on the following scriptures about obedience:

> Behold, to obey is better than sacrifice...For rebellion
> is as the sin of witchcraft.
>
> —1 SAMUEL 15:22–23

> And all these blessings shall come upon you and overtake
> you, because you obey the voice of the LORD your God.
>
> —DEUTERONOMY 28:2

Reading to verse 14 of chapter 28, excitement began
to rise in my spirit as I gained fresh insight as to why some
people have a much easier and more fulfilled life than others.
I thought about the great numbers of children I had taught,
especially the rooms full of boys and girls during the years
I did substitute teaching; the ones in constant trouble were
invariably the rebellious kids. How I regret not knowing the

wisdom of God's Holy Word at that time, so as to teach them these powerful truths. I am sure much heartbreak and many of life's disappointments could have been avoided for a great number of them. In my own life, the blessings of obedience now truly amaze me. I praise God for the example that was set, through the generations before me.

> The righteous man walks in his integrity; his children are blessed after him.
>
> —PROVERBS 20:7

My mother used to comment that I was an obedient child; she called me her little peacemaker, being the only girl between two brothers. Sunday afternoons, as mentioned earlier, my parents would get out the *Baltimore Catechism* and they frequently stressed the Ten Commandments. In spite of rattling them off, I now realize they had gone deep into my spirit, especially the one about honoring my father and mother. I attributed my obedience to fear of disobeying God and ending up in hell, and wanting to please my parents out of love and respect for them. In retrospect, I also can see the strength and power of His Word at work in my life.

A true test of my obedience occurred my sophomore year in college. I attended a girls' Catholic school and had begun to date a young man from a theater production we were both in. He attended the Catholic boys' college across town but lived in a city not far from campus. One weekend, he invited me to visit his home and meet his family. I was wishing I could go since I did like him; he was intelligent, good-looking, and talented in music, which I also enjoyed. The big problem was I didn't have permission from my parents to leave the town where the college was located. Most of the girls had written permission to go away on weekends, but this was not the case in my situation, due to such protective parents. I told the young man I could not disobey my folks, to which he replied no one would ever know; that caused great concern in my heart. I stood fast repeating that no way could I disobey.

On Sunday afternoons, after attending Mass, brunch, and study hall, we students were allowed to go to a college hangout in the town. Everyone congregated around the coke machine and put money in the jukebox so we could dance to our favorite songs. That Sunday, a tall, dark, and handsome Italian asked me to dance and then asked if he could walk me back to my campus; he also went to the boys' college in the other part of town.

Later, at dinner, there was a buzz in the dining room about someone being in an accident the night before. When I heard it was the young man I could have gone away with, I must have turned ashen during mealtime grace; everyone at my table was staring at me by the time we sat down. My heart was racing a mile a minute as I inquired about him and the accident. He had suffered serious injuries and returned to school weeks later in a partial body cast. My mind was flooded with thoughts of what if I had disobeyed my wonderful, trusting parents and also been seriously injured or possibly killed. (There were no seat belts in those days.) Disobedience would have caused untold grief for my family, the possible loss of my soul, or I could have been paralyzed and spent the rest of my life blaming God, as all too frequently happens. Instead of tragedy, the handsome young Italian that walked me home that day turned out to be my future husband and the father of our four wonderful children. I have been blessed beyond measure with long life and great happiness. This lesson in obedience has deeply impacted my life.

> Honor your father and your mother, that your days may
> be long upon the land...
>
> —Exodus 20:12

This commandment is the only one with a promise
attached to it. I am reminded of a time when I was a child
playing in the grove while my father was cutting up a fallen
tree. Mother had brought out lemonade for Dad when she let
out a scream for me to stop and stand still. I had been running
toward a favorite tree branch to swing on when she noticed
a swarm of bees on that very branch. By instant obedience,
I no doubt prolonged my life and possibly the lives of my
parents.

Another lesson in obedience was learning to tithe.

> "Will a man rob God? Yet you have robbed Me! But
> you say, 'In what way have we robbed You?' In tithes
> and offerings....Bring all the tithes into the store-
> house...And try Me now in this," Says the Lord of
> hosts, "If I will not open for you the windows of heaven
> and pour out for you such blessing that there will not be
> room enough to receive it."
>
> —Malachi 3:8, 10

The thought of robbing God greatly disturbed me. It
was also a revelation that I felt compelled to obey. I began
to tithe and send offerings, not wanting to miss any of the
blessings found in Matthew 25, where Jesus tells us when
we feed the hungry, clothe the naked, and visit the sick and
those in prison, we are doing it as unto Him. (See Matthew
25:35–40.) I sent money to a prison ministry, started support-
ing an orphan each month, sent Bibles to missionaries, and
did many more forms of giving to God's family, along with
our Sunday envelope at church. One Saturday my husband

brought in the mail and soon I heard him yell. I ran to see if one of the boys was hurt. Spread out on the table, were all the canceled checks for the month. That was one of the few times Oscar ever raised his voice at me. He announced he was just one man trying to pay tuitions for private schooling and was not able to support the entire world. I felt very repentant and sorry that I had been so thoughtless. I told him I was trying to obey God when I had read about this in His word. It didn't occur to me to check with him since he was always extremely generous. I had just assumed he'd be as happy and excited as I was to obey God's command.

> He who sows sparingly will also reap sparingly, and he who sows bountifully will also reap bountifully. So let each one give as he purposes in his heart...for God loves a cheerful giver. And God is able to make all grace abound toward you, that you, always having all sufficiency in all things, may have an abundance for every good work.
> —2 CORINTHIANS 9:6–8

Oscar firmly stressed, and rightly so, that I was not to give any more money away unless I checked with him first. I stopped everything but the church envelopes. My heart was heavy thinking about all the people that would miss our help; those checks had been my favorite ones to send.

> For where your treasure is, there your heart will be also.
> —MATTHEW 6:21

Not long after the tithing episode, there was a call from the high school asking me to come to the gym as soon as possible. Our oldest son had broken his collarbone when someone fell on him as he slid into base during a ballgame. (That was the only broken bone ever, in our household.)

One chilly evening, Oscar got out of the pool and dashed toward the house; he went through the glass patio door, thinking it was open. While he was in the hospital's emergency ward having his head and leg stitched, I sat in the waiting room questioning God as to why, all of a sudden, so many bad things were happening to our family. We were still concerned about losing the baby I was carrying; our son was healing from a broken bone; Nona was upstairs, in the same hospital, having just suffered another heart attack; and now my dear husband was suffering great pain from his dreadful open wounds. Several times the thought came that we had stepped out of God's blessing and protection through disobedience. I knew immediately we needed to begin sending tithes and offerings again.

> Therefore, to him who knows to do good and does not do it, to him it is sin.
> —James 4:17

On the way home from the hospital, Oscar said he was wondering why we were suddenly experiencing so many problems. I shared what I felt was the answer I had received while praying in the waiting room. My precious husband, still in a lot of pain, said I should go ahead with the tithes and offerings; his only condition was that I "not give away the house," which I promised I wouldn't do. The blessings that followed continue to astound all of us. God's Word is totally trustworthy, and He watches over His Word to perform it.

> So shall My word be that goes forth from My mouth;
> it shall not return to Me void, but it shall accomplish

what I please, and it shall prosper in the thing for which
I sent it.

—Isaiah 55:11

Another great blessing was obeying God to have "one more child." I enjoyed the healing of varicose veins and not one day of morning sickness, as experienced in the three previous pregnancies. This child continues to bless everyone with his charming personality and gift of music. I tell him God has big plans for his life, especially after "ordering his birth."

> Praise Him with the sound of the trumpet; praise Him
> with the lute and harp! ... praise Him with loud cymbals; praise Him with clashing symbols! Let everything
> that has breath praise the Lord. Praise the Lord!
>
> —Psalm 150:3, 5–6

With its ongoing blessings, the Love and Praise Prayer Meeting was also a result of my obedience in having "one more child." When I could no longer attend a prayer meeting due to having a new baby and later having surgery, one was brought to our home.

> Every day I will bless You, and I will praise Your name
> forever and ever.
>
> —Psalm 145:2

By obeying the Lord to have a "class on the Holy Spirit," we were blessed to meet Liz, the little girl in need of a car. Through our son's gift of a car, she met her husband. The night of their baby's birth, we met the darling nurse who had obeyed her parents by breaking up with a young man they didn't feel was right for her. She later married our son who had obeyed his parents by no longer dating a girl we felt was not right for him. Another of God's great blessings was the birth of our two beautiful granddaughters.

> Trust in the LORD with all your heart, and lean not on your own understanding; in all your ways acknowledge Him, and He shall direct your paths.
>
> —PROVERBS 3:5–6

CHAPTER 9

My Oscar

———◆◆◆———

W HEN INTRODUCING MY FIANCÉ TO MY pastor, he
remarked, in his Irish wit, that I was fortunate not to
have to go to Hollywood for my Oscar. In looking back, it
is clear Hollywood couldn't produce anything even close to
what God had blessed me with in this dear man.

Oscar and I met in college as mentioned in a previous
chapter. He was drafted into the Army shortly after his gradu-
ation. Oscar had met my parents and had asked me to marry
him to which I had replied in the affirmative. He was eager
for me to meet his parents, but Mother and Dad had forbidden me to go to the big city of Chicago alone. They both
accompanied me as we traveled by train to visit Oscar's family. We then went on to see my older brother who had been
moved to a new monastery in New York.

Later, during Christmas vacation, Oscar came to my
home supposedly to get engaged, however, he made no mention of having a ring. I was becoming apprehensive, thinking

perhaps he had changed his mind, when my younger brother, informed me he had seen the ring. One afternoon, Oscar and I stopped at my church to make a visit and as usual I lit a vigil light and prayed for God's blessings. Kneeling beside Oscar at the communion rail, I turned and noticed the lovely box containing a diamond placed at the foot of baby Jesus in front of the Christmas crèche. It was shooting rays of light as the sun shone on it through a stained glass window. He lovingly placed the ring on my finger. We embraced amid tears of joy when, suddenly, I panicked at the thought of my pastor walking in; Oscar got such a kick out of that. He said he had been praying for the right moment to give me the ring. I assured him it was the perfect moment and the perfect place. He was every bit a gentleman; always very thoughtful and such a romantic. Often, he would recite beautiful poetry when we were dancing. There was no end to my growing love and appreciation for my knight in shining armor.

We faithfully wrote daily letters the two years he was in the service, one year of which was spent in Korea. I had received my teaching certificate and was enjoying my first classroom of children in a school in Kansas at the time. On very cold days, I sometimes observed the children at recess from behind a glass door. I would watch the sun shoot colored rays off my new diamond and dream of my love so far away. Every evening, after finishing a letter to my favorite soldier, I marked off another day on the calendar until his return.

I loved being a teacher and found it very rewarding. The main topic in my letters had to do with "my kids." One little boy had been a poor student with low self-esteem. I discovered his artistic talent and asked him to do seasonal scenes with colored chalk on the back blackboard. Teachers and students from other grades would come to view, admire, and rave about his artwork. His attitude regarding school changed dramatically. His mother commented she couldn't get over how his hatred for school had now turned to love. She was thrilled at his sudden turn around.

Several teachers had previously warned me about a troublemaker the year I taught fifth grade. This became a wonderful challenge. Even then, I recognized that love never failed.

And now abide faith, hope, love, these three; but the greatest of these is love.

—1 CORINTHIANS 13:13

The first day of school that year he ran for a seat in the last row, to sit behind a large boy, so as not to be seen by the teacher. I would frequently walk around the room when giving a test or during study time. As I passed by this child, I made an extra effort to comment on his nice work and would pat him on the head or shoulder; he was the middle child in a large family and obviously not used to positive attention. Several weeks into the school year, I was surprised when he asked to trade places with a boy who sat in front of my desk; he had decided he couldn't see very well from the back of the room. I willingly obliged as some of the students gasped. He no longer bullied on the playground and the improvement in his schoolwork was nothing short of amazing. Former teachers would remark about the change in him, as they tried to figure out how this was happening. The day finally came when I felt it was safe to have him run an errand to the office and not end up on the playground or teasing someone in the hall; he could hardly believe it. With a grin from ear to ear, he swaggered out of the room, returning shortly with the same big smile and a look of great satisfaction on his darling face. He became a great student. When I returned to my home in Iowa that summer, I was thrilled to have a letter from him already waiting for me. He was begging me to be his teacher the following year. What joy and satisfaction that letter gave me!

Give, and it will be given to you...

—LUKE 6:38

Oscar enjoyed my "teacher stories" and I eagerly read his fascinating tales of being a member of the military police in Korea. He often shared how he prayed, especially in dangerous situations and seldom missed saying the rosary. I, too, prayed the rosary daily and never missed morning Mass asking God's protection for him. He wrote what a letdown it was when he didn't receive a letter at mail call. All was well the next day, however, when two or three arrived. He told about a fellow in his tent dashing out the door, into the pouring rain, after reading a letter. Oscar followed the loud sobs to the back of the hut where he discovered that the soldier's wife had sent a "Dear John," saying she had found someone else and wanted a divorce. This really impacted Oscar's tender heart. He tried to comfort the young man and prayed that he himself would never experience such heartbreak.

I had taken a teaching job in my home town to be near my parents before getting married. During this time, Dad asked me to write and see if Oscar would be interested in farming after he got out of the army, since he and Mother were ready to retire. In my heart, I knew he couldn't bear the thought of his little girl moving to another state. I had a good chuckle at the idea of my city-boy farmer, but obeyed Dad's request. To the surprise of all of us, Oscar wrote back saying he would love to try his hand at farming.

Upon receiving that news, a busy and exciting time followed. My parents bought a home in a nearby town. I helped with painting and decorating that house and also prepared the home I grew up in, for Oscar and me. Together with teaching sixth grade, my parents move, and making wedding preparations, the weeks simply flew by. Soon, the long-anticipated day finally arrived.

What a happy homecoming we had! I remember being very nervous and praying we would still feel the same love for each other, after having been apart for almost a year. Once Oscar enfolded me in his strong arms, I wanted to stay there forever and knew this was God's answer to our many prayers.

Call to Me, and I will answer you...
—JEREMIAH 33:3

I refer to this verse as God's phone number and use it often. The line is always available and the answer is usually a simple "Yes," "No," or "Later."

We were married before Lent, due to the church's regulations at that time of no weddings during the Lenten Season, and also so that Oscar could begin farming in early spring. I had the thrill of my first plane ride when we went to Miami Beach for our honeymoon. Afterward, we were both on cloud nine as Oscar carried me over the threshold of our first home, the one I had grown up in.

We later both agreed that that was probably one of the best years of our lives. Oscar met all of my extended family and he became acquainted with everyone I had grown up with. He especially enjoyed meeting my sixth-grade class and could see firsthand how fond I was of each one of those thirty-six kids. Oscar loved to read, and read most of the books from the town library. On one occasion, he shared his disgust after asking the librarian for a book on farming. When he told her he couldn't find one, she burst out laughing. Hearing this, I couldn't help but stifle a giggle. It then dawned on him how amusing his question must have seemed, in such a farming community. He began to roar with laughter saying he bet that was the first time she had ever had that request in her little library.

He was determined to show those big farmers he was no city-boy weakling. On the coldest of days, when no one was out, Oscar would put on his army parka, boots, and gloves and head for the field. He was in his glory as he drove the tractor preparing the soil for planting. The town gossip would frequently drive by to see how the Chicago boy was faring. Oscar was amused when Dad told him the people around town were talking about how tough he was to be out in such weather.

I still remember nearly falling over with laughter when he first tried to milk a cow. I was no help. Dad felt that the barn was no place for ladies; consequently, Mother and I had never learned to milk. Early one morning, after milking, Oscar spotted a newborn calf out in the pasture. He was afraid it would freeze so he picked it up and carried it to the warmth of the barn. I'm not sure he realized the danger he was in with the nervous mother following so closely behind him. This also caused a local stir since the town gossip just happened to be driving by once again and raved about the strength of the city boy.

Dad thoroughly enjoyed Oscar and frequently commented on how fast he moved. This was in direct contrast to Dad, who moved at a much slower pace. One day during harvest, when filling a bin with corn, the elevator began to tip toward Dad. Oscar saved Dad's life by pulling him out of the way before the large machine crashed to the ground, landing on the very spot where Dad had been working. We were all most grateful for Oscar's alertness and rapid movements. Attempting to brag on my new husband, I remarked that Oscar's speed no doubt explained his trophies for ping pong, boxing, basketball, and handball. Not to be outdone, Dad then joked that when he played football the other team just sat down once he had the ball; he was so fast they knew they could never catch him. Everyone had a good laugh at that tall tale.

On rainy days when they couldn't be in the fields, the two of them would spend hours in conversation while I was teaching. Dad would argue there was no way a man would ever walk on the moon. Oscar was positive, however, that Dad would live to see it. When it did happen, Dad remarked that no generation had ever experienced the progress his age group had seen. He would contrast horse and buggy rides with a rocket ship to the moon. Later, as this topic, along with the wonder of the computer age, would arise, a verse from the book of Daniel would come to mind.

> But you, Daniel, shut up the words, and seal the book until the time of the end; many shall run to and fro, and knowledge shall increase.
>
> —DANIEL 12:4

A great blessing that year for the two of us was visiting a darling little girl who had been stricken with polio. When I began teaching in my hometown, I drove by a house where this little girl would be out for fresh air, sitting in her wheelchair. I always waved and noticed her fingers move in response. One day, I went to the school principal to ask about her. He informed me she was physically unable to attend classes due to polio; he lamented the fact there were no funds available for a tutor. I said I would be happy to stop and teach her since I drove by every day. He reminded me there would be no pay, to which I said I didn't care; no longer could I just drive by. That was the beginning of a love affair for all of us. Jenny was extremely bright and sailed through third grade in three months. It was fun to work with her since she was so eager and willing to learn and was such a doll. There were pictures of her looking like Shirley Temple before being stricken with polio. Oscar also loved this little girl and on occasion, when picking me up, would bring her candy bars and pictures of Elvis, her favorite singer.

One evening the following year, we had a frantic call from Oscar's mother saying his dad had had a heart attack. She begged us to move near to them. Being the only child, Oscar felt that was what we must do. Dad was able to make other arrangements regarding the farm. I hadn't signed up for another year of teaching, hoping to start a family; by then we were both elated to finally be expecting our first child. I did substitute teach and continued tutoring our little friend, Jenny. We were now faced with the dilemma as to what to do about this bright little girl. Talking to the principal, I discovered that by going to the state capitol, arrangements could be made to have a speaker set up from the classroom to her home, thus enabling her to continue her education. Oscar had researched this, so we excitedly set out for Des Moines. We were thrilled to learn it would not be difficult to have the speaker system set up for Jenny.

Jenny went on to graduate from high school, marry a local boy, have two sons, and is now the proud grandmother of five. She travels the country speaking from her wheelchair for people with disabilities, stressing the need for handicapped improvements. In 2004 she hosted the 31st National Ms. Wheelchair America Pageant, held in Des Moines, and has served as state coordinator for the past seven years. We continue to correspond at Christmastime. What an amazing woman she is!

After our move to Chicago, Oscar and I stayed with his parents for several months until we found a house we liked and could afford. This was a great opportunity for me to learn about Oscar's family and meet his friends. His dad was doing well after his heart attack, and both parents were very warm and loving; they could hardly contain their excitement over a grandbaby. Soon we were all overjoyed at the birth of our son. On the way home from the hospital, to the house we had recently purchased in Oak Park, Oscar remarked we had better pray that the baby stay healthy. We had just passed the bank where he was reminded that we had less than ten dollars in our account. Alarmed, I asked how that could be. He confessed he hadn't thought to buy maternity insurance and had to pay a lot more than he had anticipated to get us out of the hospital. I remember being very frugal so as to make those house payments. I wouldn't indulge even in a candy bar. The small sacrifice was well worth it. We never paid a rent check, which made a fantastic difference in our lives, adding numerous blessings over the years.

Oscar took a job in sales and one of the business machines he sold was called the 209. He did so well selling to major accounts in downtown Chicago he was named "King of the 209's." We were always amazed at how often that number came up in our lives. My parents lived at 209 North Walnut, one of our hotel rooms in Hawaii was 209, and a flight number to a vacation had been 209. The day we sold Oscar's share of his company, after his death, I just happened to notice the mileage on my car turn to 209 as I pulled in front of the office. That same day, I was with our oldest son to deposit a check from the sale and was telling him about this. Together, we looked down and almost in unbelief, we watched the mileage meter in his car turn to 209 the moment we stopped in front of the bank. We were twice blessed since this seemed to be confirmation that we had done the right thing. Whenever I see 2:09 on the clock, especially in the night, my thoughts turn heavenward. I am filled with thanksgiving for God's many blessings, even to His getting our attention in the simplest of ways. Amazing! Just now, while writing this, I had the urge to check Psalm 20:9 and was blessed to read: "Save, Lord! May the King answer us when we call."

> Through the Lord's mercies we are not consumed, because His compassions fail not. They are new every morning; great is Your faithfulness.
> —Lamentations 3:22–23

Spending a weekend at the ocean, Oscar and I had walked along the beach on our way to breakfast. After leaving the restaurant and leisurely strolling on the same path back to our hotel, we joined many others in reading the words that had been written in huge letters in the sand: EVERY KNEE SHALL BOW AND EVERY TONGUE CONFESS JESUS CHRIST IS LORD OF LORDS AND KING OF KINGS. We commented that someone must have done that while we were eating, since it wasn't there when we went into the restaurant. Arriving back in our hotel room, Oscar randomly opened the Bible and began to read:

> Therefore God also has highly exalted Him and given Him the name which is above every name, that at the name of Jesus every knee should bow, of those in heaven, and of those on earth, and of those under the earth, and that every tongue should confess that Jesus Christ is Lord, to the glory of God the Father.
> —Philippians 2:9–11

He gave a shout and began to read the passage out loud to me; he was amazed to have opened to the same message we had just seen written in the sand. Rejoicing, I couldn't help but tease him about enjoying the blessings of "Bible roulette" like his wacky wife.

During a trip to Hawaii, Oscar was thrilled to run across an old friend he used to work with. He remarked how well he looked and his friend said he attributed that to spending fifteen minutes a day hating their former boss. We used to go to office parties with him and his wife and I knew this man regularly attended church. I laughingly said I hoped he no longer prayed the "Our Father." He grew quite serious and asked, "Why not?" I reminded him that Jesus said He would forgive us as we forgave others.

And forgive us our debts, as we forgive our debtors.
—MATTHEW 6:12

No longer joking, he responded that was really food for thought; his wife gave me a wink and a grin. Oscar gave a big chuckle; I was relieved I hadn't upset either of them.

We were driving to a party one evening when Oscar asked me to say a prayer that he would find his billfold. My reaction was to ask the Holy Spirit, who leads us in all truth, to please bring to mind where it was. Before I finished praying, he reached under the seat and brought out his wallet. He had driven to the college track for a run a couple of days earlier and had forgotten that he had placed it under the seat.

Before they call, I will answer; and while they are still speaking, I will hear.
—ISAIAH 65:24

A story Oscar enjoyed telling was that of being pulled over by a patrolman for speeding, as we were rushing to a wedding. Lucy, a dear friend, had given him a copy of the book *Good News for Modern Man* to keep in the car to read when he was stuck in traffic. Upon opening the glove compartment for the car registration, I left the book on the open glove compartment door. The patrolman spotted it and asked if Oscar was a Christian, to which he unhesitatingly responded that he was. The officer said he was also a Christian and wouldn't give him a ticket for speeding if he promised to slow down and keep reading the Good Book, to which Oscar readily agreed.

Oscar also liked to tell his young salespeople the following story: An old Indian chief was walking with a young brave. The brave remarked he sometimes felt as though there were two wolves fighting inside his head. The chief asked if he would like to know which one won. The young man nodded in the affirmative. The chief wisely told him, "The one you feed the most." Oscar dearly loved his salespeople and had great concern when he saw one of them going the wrong way in life. Often, taking my hand, he would suggest that we pray together for whoever it was that had a need.

> Again I say to you that if two of you agree on earth concerning anything that they ask, it will be done for them by My Father in heaven.
> —Matthew 18:19

Some of the favorite times spent with my husband and best friend were the long walks we frequently took. We would praise and thank God for blessing us with our three special sons, wonderful daughter-in-law, and precious granddaughters. Observing the beauty of the Master's creation all around us, we expressed our appreciation by thanking Him numerous times for the transfer to California. On one occasion, Oscar remarked our lives were going so well it was almost frightening. We both acknowledged that the closer we walked to the Lord, the more we experienced His blessings.

> But seek first the kingdom of God and His righteousness, and all these things shall be added to you.
> —MATTHEW 6:33

In 1991, after a family cookout on the Fourth of July, our nurse daughter-in-law remarked that Oscar didn't look well; she helped convince him to go to the doctor for a checkup. I understood his hesitancy about seeing a doctor, since his only sickness in our thirty-five years of marriage had been two cases of the flu. He did call the family physician only to discover he was on vacation. Because Oscar was very tired and had a pain on his left side, I suggested he call my heart specialist, which he did. He was eager to get to the bottom of this, especially since his father had died of a sudden heart attack in his early sixties.

On July thirteenth, Oscar had an appointment to receive the results of an MRI the doctor had ordered. I was afraid he might need gall bladder surgery like Mother had recently, since the symptoms sounded similar. My first question when he came home was regarding an operation. He grabbed my hand tightly in his and led me to the couch where he told me he would not need surgery. The doctor informed him he had pancreatic cancer with a possible three to six months to live. We clung to each other sobbing uncontrollably at the unbelievable and dreadful news. The doctor had said there was no known cure and suggested he surround himself with those he loved, and if he wanted to travel, to do so immediately while he still had the strength. My first thought was such a selfish one of how could I ever go on without my partner and best friend? Then I realized what Oscar must be going through. It was simply overwhelming!

Our youngest son came dashing in from work shouting a quick "Hi" and not to fix dinner for him as he had a date with a beautiful blonde. Drying our tears, we decided not to ruin his evening. Soon our oldest son called to hear the results of Dad's tests. He and his wife and babies came over immediately. I'll never forget that embrace of Oscar and his firstborn son; I can feel the pain even today.

Later that evening, we shared the heartbreaking news with our youngest son. All we could do was hold on to each other and weep; that night all of our pillows were soaked with tears.

The following day we knew we had to call our middle son who was in Washington, DC, for the summer. Oscar wanted to wait and tell him when he came home in a few weeks. He was very concerned about how he would handle this without family support. We convinced Oscar it wasn't right to not inform him. Like the rest of us, he was devastated at the news. Fortunately, he had a dinner date planned with a girl who was very understanding. She had just experienced her mother having cancer, but due to therapy, she was getting better.

The next week we had an appointment with an oncologist. He presented the x-rays and stated my husband only had two months to live. I had the peace that passes understanding, even at hearing this horrible news. In my heart I was confident of God's miracle-working power. By this time, I had called every prayer chain and praying person I knew to intercede for my beloved Oscar's miracle. I was memorizing scriptures on healing and reminding God of His promises day and night.

> Be anxious for nothing, but in everything by prayer
> and supplication, with thanksgiving, let your requests
> be made known to God; and the peace of God, which
> surpasses all understanding, will guard your hearts and
> minds through Christ Jesus.
>
> —PHILIPPIANS 4:6–7

Oscar bravely kept going to work; I had never known him to miss a day, ever. The strain was evident as he tried so desperately to keep up; finally, he was forced to admit he didn't have the strength to make it to the office. One evening, he made an unusual request asking me to drive him to his office; he had always driven when we were together. My heart sank recalling the oncologist's prediction about his not feeling up to driving. Arm in arm and through our tears we watched our last beautiful sunset together. His appetite began to decrease. Soon, he could not bear the smell of food cooking. As if on cue, prepared meals began arriving at our door from many sisters in the Lord.

Years ago, Oscar had had a life-changing experience at a prayer meeting when visiting my parents in Iowa. Someone had read:

> For the hearts of this people have grown dull. Their ears
> are hard of hearing, And their eyes they have closed,
> Lest they should see with their eyes and hear with their
> ears, Lest they should understand with their hearts and
> turn, so that I should heal them. But blessed are your
> eyes for they see, and your ears for they hear; for assur-
> edly, I say to you that many prophets and righteous men
> desired to see what you see, and did not see it, and to
> hear what you hear, and did not hear it.
>
> —MATTHEW 13:11, 15–16

He later said that upon hearing this scripture he did understand with his heart and had totally turned to Jesus. After coming home from that trip, he sat out on the diving board by the pool for a long time. Later, he said the presence of God was so strong he asked it to stop as he couldn't take anymore. I regret that I didn't ask him to explain that further.

The days were now filled with prayer, watching Christian TV, and reading God's Word. Not once did Oscar grumble or ask, "Why me?" He jokingly said he guessed God finally had his full attention, now that he was flat on his back and recalled Saint Augustine's saying, "Our hearts are restless till they rest in Thee, O Lord." He did say the only good thing about cancer was that it gave one time to prepare to meet his Maker. I watched him go from a busy executive to a man after God's own heart. The doctor had given him pain medicine which made him sick. After two days, he refused to take it saying he didn't need it. He would read Scripture and then lay the Bible across his stomach and, with a twinkle in his eye, remind me there was healing in God's Word. I had memorized Psalm 23 and Psalm 91 which were his favorites. Again and again he would ask me to repeat those beautiful reassuring words. My faith remained high as I continued to trust God for our miracle.

One Sunday, as our youngest son and I were going to Mass, the assistant pastor met us at the door. I asked him to remember Oscar in his prayers as he had been diagnosed with pancreatic cancer. He asked if that wasn't what Michael Landon, the TV actor, had recently died with. When I said it was, he took my hand in his and with the compassion of Jesus assured us of his prayers. We were very blessed over this young priest's concern.

Because Oscar was too weak to attend Mass, I would bring the Eucharist home to him. On one occasion, he asked me to sit for a minute before preparing lunch. He had the sweetest expression I had ever seen. He proceeded to tell me Jesus had been there. Awestruck, I asked what He said. Oscar replied, "He stood right here by the piano and just smiled at me." With his face all aglow he said, "Joan, I want to go Home." In spite of that holy moment, I felt sick inside. I realized by the look on Oscar's face there was no holding him on this earth.

Later I phoned Dottie, a dear prayer partner, who often prayed the nights through. Trying to suppress the tears, I related Jesus' visit to Oscar. She began to pray in the power of the Spirit and then said, "Now Joan, this is not between you and Oscar or even between you and God. This is between Oscar and his God; don't you dare stand in the way of what God is doing." I told her how I was praying and trusting for his miracle. Hearing the anguish in my voice, she knew this needed to be dealt with. She suggested that we pray together. She asked me to place my will for him to be healed on the altar and then for Oscar to put his desire to go Home on the altar of the Lord. Then, having done that, to release it to the Father, trusting in His perfect will to be done. I hung up the phone, dried my tears, and went to Oscar's bedside. After I explained my phone call, we held hands and prayed, releasing our wills to our heavenly Father and asking for His perfect plan to unfold. The moment we finished praying, I felt as though a huge weight had lifted from me and will never forget the look of peace on my dear husband's face. It was even more difficult than usual to get to sleep that night. I continued praying in the Holy Spirit for I didn't know how to pray.

> Likewise the Spirit also helps in our weaknesses. For we
> do not know what we should pray for as we ought, but

the Spirit Himself makes intercession for us with groanings which cannot be uttered.

—Romans 8:26

During this time of intercession there was almost an audible voice that said: "The twenty-eighth is to be Oscar's glory day." I had never heard that expression, but realized what it could mean. Continuing to pray in tongues, the same thought would come again and again. I decided to ask our dear pastor what he thought about it the next time he brought communion to Oscar. He looked puzzled and said he had not heard this phrase before either. I continued to ponder: "The twenty-eighth is to be Oscar's glory day."

Oscar was failing rapidly. The doctor suggested I call Hospice. Soon a nurse came with instructions on how to care for him and cope with the inevitable. She had been doing hospice work for over ten years and commented she had never seen anyone so ready to meet his God. She informed me this would be an easy transition; he would probably go into a coma and slip on over to the other side.

After she left, I fell to my knees crying as though my heart would burst. I begged God for two favors. First, to keep Oscar from a coma, as that had happened to our little Mary Bernadette, which terrified us; and second, that I might be holding his hand when He came for him. Again, almost audibly, I then heard: "I am coming for Oscar at about the eleventh hour." My mind was flooded with: "The twenty-eighth is to be Oscar's glory day," and now: "I am coming for Oscar at about the eleventh hour." I began to wonder if I was imagining all this due to stress or exhaustion. I realized the answer to everything was to keep on praying in the Holy Spirit, trusting He would lead us in all truth as His Word promised.

However, when He, the Spirit of truth, has come, He will guide you into all truth...

—JOHN 16:13

The scripture that became my lifeline was:

And He said to me, "My grace is sufficient for you, for My strength is made perfect in weakness."

—2 CORINTHIANS 12:9

I rarely left Oscar's side. We prayed, cried, and laughed remembering all the good times we had shared, always counting our many blessings. My heart is still full of his wonderful words of affirmation and encouragement. He said he didn't understand it, but he knew it was his time to go Home. Between sobs, he would say how hard it was to leave his wonderful family, but he was most eager to be with Jesus and to see little Mary Bernadette again. He took great comfort in my strong faith. Then he stunned me by saying he felt God had something for me to do and he would be in the way of that. When I questioned him about its meaning, he smiled sweetly saying he really didn't understand it, but someday I would know what it meant. I'm still wondering what that could be.

His last advice to our three wonderful sons, as they gathered around his bed, was to remind them how hard he had worked and the money he had made, stressing he wasn't taking a penny with him. He told them, in the end, nothing else mattered but to have a close walk with Jesus Christ. I'm sure that powerful moment was etched in their memories forever.

As he came from his mother's womb, naked shall he return, to go as he came; and he shall take nothing from his labor which he may carry away in his hand.

—ECCLESIASTES 5:15

The night of August twenty-seventh, Oscar needed pain pills for the first time due to the excruciating pain. I called the doctor. Our oldest son, who had come to spend the night, went for medicine at midnight. It was heart wrenching to see my strong, macho man in such pain. Prayer was unceasing!

August twenty-eighth, while cleaning the kitchen after breakfast and in constant prayer, I reminded the Holy Spirit what day it was; I asked if Jesus was coming for Oscar in the am or pm. Immediately the thought came: "I am coming very soon for Oscar." I rushed to his bedside, knelt, and began to recite his favorite Psalms. I knocked on the adjoining wall for our middle son, recently home from Washington, DC, to come get on his knees, as Jesus was coming soon for Dad. When praying, we could see the suffering and anguish on his dear face. I was overcome with the desire to relieve him; I heard myself ask the Father not to let him suffer. I prayed: "Lord Jesus, come with Your angels and saints to take Oscar safely home. I release him to you." Oscar gently squeezed my hand, gave a weak smile and whispered, "I love you," as his spirit went into the loving arms of his Jesus. I carefully closed his beautiful brown eyes and kissed him for the last time. I had received my miracle!

> For I consider that the sufferings of this present time are not worthy to be compared with the glory which shall be revealed in us.
> —ROMANS 8:18

By God's wonderful grace, our middle son made calls to our oldest son who had gone to the office, the parish priest, and the hospice nurse. Our youngest son was buying books to begin his senior year of high school and would be home shortly.

There was a knock at the door as our dear pastor, Father

Cottrell, arrived. I told him Oscar had just gone home to Glory. He ran down the hall and began giving him the last rites of the church. Father then said he would like a word with me. He asked when Oscar told me his "glory day" would be the twenty-eighth, reminding me it was indeed the twenty-eighth. I told him I frequently heard the statement in my prayer time but had never mentioned it to Oscar. He said it was the feast of Saint Augustine, to which I replied that was one of Oscar's favorite saints. Just then the hospice nurse came and I was reminded to tell Father about the most recent thought that recurred while praying in the Spirit, of Jesus coming for Oscar at about the eleventh hour. Looking at the grandfather clock, noticing it was a few minutes past eleven, his blue eyes opened wide as he shared his amazement, stating he had been a priest for forty years and had never experienced anything like this. While we were talking, the nurse put some forms on the table and let herself out. After Father left, I checked the form on which she had written the time of death; it read, 11 am on August 28, 1991. Our middle son had noticed the time when Oscar died was 10:44 am. (Later this son needed his birth certificate and was surprised to see that he was born at 10:44 am; different day and year of course, but reassuring that God knows the hour and minute of our coming and our going.)

> ...And in Your book they all were written, the days fashioned for me...
>
> —Psalm 139:16

Oh the sting of death! One of the lowest moments of my life was watching the lifeless body of my wonderful partner and very best friend on this earth, being carried from our home. It was difficult to grasp that our thirty-five-and-a-half years of life together had come to an end. What a marvelous chapter it had been and what a wonderful legacy Oscar had left in his three outstanding sons.

> Behold, children are a heritage from the Lord...
>
> —Psalm 127:3

The morning after Oscar's home-going, Jane, a prayerful Aglow sister, called very excited to tell me that in her prayer time she was given a mental picture of Oscar swinging a little girl around. She knew we had lost our daughter, but no way could she ever have known that was their routine. Hearing Oscar's key in the door, Mary would run to him throwing up her little arms shouting, "Da dee, Da dee," as he picked her up and swung her around. I could hardly contain the heart-break of having both of them gone, yet there was a part of my heart that was rejoicing at their happiness, and knowing someday we would all be together forever.

> Let not your heart be troubled; you believe in God, believe also in Me. In My Father's house are many man-sions; if it were not so, I would have told you. I go to prepare a place for you. And if I go and prepare a place for you, I will come again and receive you to Myself; that where I am, there you may be also.
>
> —John 14:1–3

We read in Sirach it is good to mourn.

> My son, shed tears for one who is dead with wail-ing and bitter lament. As is only proper, prepare the body, absent not yourself from his burial; weeping bitterly, mourning fully, pay your tribute of sorrow, as he deserves.
>
> —Sirach 38:16–17, nas

Attending a wake and funeral Mass was an important part in the healing process; there was great comfort and consolation in such an outpouring of love and sympathy. All three sons took part in the funeral service. God's grace and strength was evident as each one paid tribute to the Father they so cherished and appreciated. I could feel the prayers of praying family and friends.

Bert and Ruth, a dear brother and sister in the Lord, organized a wonderful meal back at the house after the funeral. The numerous acts of kindness and support were blessings we will never forget. Our entire family felt privileged to be a part of God's family, the body of Christ.

After the demands of the funeral, the relatives had gone, and life somewhat returned to normal, we all realized that never again would our home be as we had known it. Our hearts ached at the vacant place at the table, the lack of Dad's stimulating conversation, and the darkened light over Oscar's favorite chair. Waves of nausea swept over me as I entered our bedroom. One night as I prayed, tossed, and turned, I felt impressed to look to my left. A full moon was shining behind a telephone pole forming a cross directly across Oscar's pillow. I had never noticed this before nor have I seen it since. The presence of my Lord gently assured me that He would always be there to help me carry this cross.

> Surely He has borne our griefs And carried our sorrows...
>
> —ISAIAH 53:4

The sickening grief seemed to lift when I released it to my wonderful, caring, heavenly Father. I took great comfort in reading:

For your Maker is your husband, the LORD of hosts is
His name.

—ISAIAH 54:5

One day, when cleaning boxes from Oscar's office, a
small piece of paper floated to the floor. Picking it up, I read:
"Joan, I love you. —Oscar." Little blessings like this seemed
like gems from heaven.

Sometime later, when awakened from a sound sleep, I
once again recognized the wonderful, sweet presence of my
Lord and began to pray in the Spirit. Soon I was given a mental picture of myself at the farm where I grew up. I was standing on an incline overlooking fields of golden grain waving in
the breeze. The fields suddenly stretched as far as I could see;
it was like trying to look across the ocean. Awestruck at this
sight, I heard that loving, familiar voice say: "The fields are
ready to harvest; will you help bring in My Father's harvest?"
Overcome with emotion at His request, all I could utter,
through my tears, was a feeble, "Yes, my Lord." I then wondered if this could possibly pertain to Oscar's saying God still
had something for me to do for Him.

Behold, I say to you, lift up your eyes and look at the
fields, for they are already white for harvest!

—JOHN 4:35

CHAPTER 10

Holy Spirit Manifestations

———◆———

And He said to them, "Go into all the world and preach the gospel to every creature. He who believes and is baptized will be saved; but he who does not believe will be condemned. And these signs will follow those who believe: In My name they will cast out demons; they will speak with new tongues... they will lay hands on the sick, and they will recover."

—Mark 16:15–18

Behold, I send the Promise of My Father upon you; but tarry in the city of Jerusalem until you are endued with power from on high.

—Luke 24:49

JESUS' LAST REQUEST BEFORE LEAVING THIS earth was for His apostles to tarry in Jerusalem until they were endued with power from on high. That Promise from the Father was the sending of His Holy Spirit as we read in Acts 1:8:

> But you shall receive power when the Holy Spirit has come upon you; and you shall be witnesses to Me in Jerusalem, and in all Judea and Samaria, and to the end of the earth.

How *important* this last instruction of Jesus was, and what a different world we would have if we obeyed that instruction to wait until we were empowered by His Holy Spirit before trying to minister in His name.

Paul asked in Ephesus, "Did you receive the Holy Spirit when you believed?"(Acts 19:2). They had not even heard there was a Holy Spirit. Yet, "when Paul had laid hands on them, the Holy Spirit came upon them, and they spoke with tongues and prophesied" (Acts 19:6).

The nine gifts of the Holy Spirit listed in 1 Corinthians 12:8–10 are: wisdom, knowledge, faith, gifts of healing, working of miracles, prophecy, discerning of spirits, different kinds of tongues, and interpretation of tongues. The gift of tongues seems to be the most maligned of all the gifts. However, my experience has been that total surrender to and reliance on the Holy Spirit to pray through me acts like the key to open the other gifts. The enemy of our souls would try to rob us of all the gifts through making such mockery of this gift. It is a powerful tool to be used for God's glory and the good of the body of Christ. Once one has experienced this, no one can convince him it is not for today or that it was done away with after the time of the apostles. I compare it to trying to convince Neil Armstrong that he did not actually walk on the moon. Frequently, the question is asked as to whether the use of tongues is of the devil. My answer is that it could be, since he can counterfeit many things. It is good to acknowledge, though, that one can only counterfeit from the original. This is where the gift of discernment is needed. The Spirit in me becomes alarmed and grieved when this wonderful Holy Spirit blessing is attributed to the evil one.

> Therefore I say to you, every sin and blasphemy will be forgiven men, but the blasphemy against the Spirit will not be forgiven men.
>
> —MATTHEW 12:31

I pray for the gentle, loving conviction of the Holy Spirit on those who do not understand or would mimic this very special gift. Using this gift as a prayer language, I finally grasp what St. Paul meant when he concluded his teaching on the whole armor of God with: "praying always with all prayer and supplication in the Spirit" (Eph. 6:18).

In Jude, verse 20, we read: "But you, beloved, building yourselves up on your most holy faith, praying in the Holy Spirit." Years ago, we called to have a large, dying tree removed from our front yard. I remember hearing the tree trimmers arrive and watching as a man was raised to the top of the tree. I turned to tend to something on the stove and after what seemed like an instant, returned to the window. To my amazement the tree was completely down. The immediate thought was that their efficiency was due to the use of proper tools. I then was reminded of how quickly and effectively work for the kingdom of God could be done if only we used His power tools, the gifts of the Holy Spirit. An instant replay began to run through my mind. I thought of the many Holy Spirit manifestations in our prayer group with the healing of kidney stones, asthma, cancer, back problems, depression, gambling, and my own healing of bone spurs in my heels, varicose veins, and morning sickness. Also, my friend's years of cigarette smoking was instantly healed and marriages were restored. The Holy Spirit can accomplish in a split second what doctors and therapists often cannot do in many years. The following scripture resonated in my mind:

> Most assuredly, I say to you, he who believes in Me, the works that I do he will do also; and greater works than these he will do, because I go to My Father. And whatever you ask in My name, that I will do, that the Father may be glorified in the Son. If you ask anything in My name, I will do it.
>
> —John 14:12–14

I had experienced some frustration, after my baptism in the Holy Spirit, due to receiving just one sentence in an unknown tongue. This was embarrassing, especially when a well-meaning lady frequently inquired about my prayer language only to discover it still consisted of a single phrase. She was concerned there must be sin in my life which added to my exasperation since I had confessed every wrong I could think of. Three or four years later, when kneeling in prayer, a whole language began to come forth accompanied with mental pictures. There was great joy and thanksgiving in my heart for the release of this wonderful Holy Spirit gift; it has been used over the years to bless many in the body of Christ. In retrospect, I can see where my doubt and a feeling of unworthiness blocked the release of this great gift and mighty tool of the Holy Spirit.

One of my first experiences in using this marvelous gift happened when I was interceding for my older brother. A mental picture came of a man struggling to climb a hill while desperately trying to balance two stacks of books with his chin. As he drew closer, I recognized my brother who had recently earned a PhD. The immediate thought was to tell Paul to forsake all books for ONE.

> Of making many books there is no end, and much study is wearisome to the flesh...Fear God and keep His commandments, for this is man's all.
> —ECCLESIASTES 12:12–13

When praying about this, I realized the more he told me about reading the writings of liberal theologians like Hans Küng, Karl Rahner, and Edward Schillebeeckx, the more confused he was becoming, even to admitting he thought he was turning into an atheist. I had suggested he read *A Crisis of Truth* by Ralph Martin, *A New Pentecost?* by Cardinal Suenens, or *Mere Christianity* by C.S. Lewis. Feeling great concern for him, I made the mistake of sharing the mental picture in a letter which understandably wasn't well received. Sometime later, after a lengthy phone conversation where my scholarly brother was reprimanding me for sounding like a fundamentalist, I went to my prayer closet and fell on my knees beseeching God as to how to pray away his skepticism and growing unbelief in God's Word. Clearly, I heard, "All Paul needs is his L.C." I was curious as to what that meant and realized he didn't yet have those initials behind his name. I then heard, "Does not My Word state that unless you become as a little child you will not enter the kingdom of heaven?"

> Assuredly, I say to you, whoever does not receive the kingdom of God as a little child will by no means enter it.
> —LUKE 18:17

Many years later, on the night of Oscar's funeral, Paul remarked how touched he was when Father Cottrell commented on Oscar's faith being the kind that was caught, not taught. It was then that I was able to share the above. A precious moment followed when, with tears in his eyes, he declared he needed to work on his "L.C." He then shared about a great encounter he had had with the Lord, when visiting the Holy Land with a group led by Mitch Pacwa, S.J. They had renewed their baptismal vows in the Jordan River, and Paul said he felt as though an enormous weight had been lifted from him as he came out of the water. He was very impressed and blessed by Father Mitch's solid walk of faith.

Later, I discovered a book by Mitch Pacwa, S.J., entitled *Catholics and the New Age*.[1] He was a professor of sacred scripture at Loyola University in Chicago. Father Pacwa, a brilliant Jesuit, backs up his teachings on the dangers of Jungian psychology, the Enneagram, Hinduism, astrology, and various New Age teachings with the truth of God's Word. He states the mantra is a short phrase or word from Hindu scriptures that is repeated many times to empty the mind or to raise one's vibration levels and unite a person to the gods. (Hindu polytheism has up to 330 million gods.) He wisely admonishes: "Like bank tellers who learn to detect counterfeit money by becoming experts at handling real money, we will detect false doctrine most easily when we become more familiar with the real thing." This book is a "must read" for anyone hungering for truth!

Another early manifestation of the Holy Spirit occurred after a Monday night prayer meeting. A lady asked for prayer for her son but didn't mention what his need was. I was among the group praying for her and began to have a mental picture of horses running around a race track. I hesitated to say anything because it seemed so strange. When this image stayed in my mind, I whispered to her what I was seeing and asked if it had any meaning. She burst into tears as she told me he had a problem with gambling on the horse races and was about to lose everything. We then prayed that the good Lord would take away his desire to gamble. She was greatly blessed and comforted as she realized how much God loved her son by revealing his problem to a complete stranger.

When praying with a Jesuit priest and prayer team, after a beautiful healing Mass, a dear soul came to us in tears and with a list of serious problems. She had breast cancer, her husband had had a heart attack, and their son was in a recent car accident. During silent prayer in tongues, a mental picture came to me of her struggling under a thick, heavy wooden cross. Suddenly, the cross turned a silver color; I asked the Holy Spirit what that meant. The immediate thought was to ask her to give these troubles to Jesus and He would cause that heavy cross to become as light as aluminum. The scripture that came to mind was: "Come to Me, all you who labor and are heavy laden, and I will give you rest....For My yoke is easy and My burden is light" (Matt. 11:28, 30). After sharing this, it was encouraging to see the sorrow and sadness in her face change to an expression of peace and hope. She had experienced a touch from the Comforter.

A wonderful manifestation of God's Spirit came the night of our oldest son's senior prom. I was awakened by a shaking on my right shoulder; my husband was asleep on my left. I looked across the hall to see if our son was home. Seeing his bedroom door open, I felt an urgency to pray. I began to pray in the Spirit, and in so doing, had a vivid picture of two sets of headlights approaching each other. I knew our son was in trouble and prayed till I felt peace and then fell back to sleep. The following morning, at the breakfast table, we inquired about the dance. The main excitement was about a car going the wrong way on the highway as he and his date were coming home. Our son felt the urge to move over a lane and then another lane. Suddenly, he saw a car with lights flashing, going the wrong direction in the lane where they had just been traveling. I then recalled the two sets of headlights and realized why I had been awakened from a sound sleep to pray. Our hearts were full of thanksgiving for God's care and mercy. I couldn't praise the Lord enough for His gift of praying in tongues and the grace to heed His warning.

> Likewise the Spirit also helps in our weaknesses. For we do not know what we should pray for as we ought, but the Spirit Himself makes intercession for us with groanings which cannot be uttered.
>
> —Romans 8:26

This same son was driving home from a day of surfing at the beach when he heard an audible voice tell him, "Slow down." Obeying, he applied the brakes as he came around a sharp turn, thus enabling him to avoid being part of an accident that had just occurred. Oscar asked if someone had warned him from a hilltop, to which he replied how unlikely that would have been; his friends were talking, the radio was on, and the windows were up. Once again, I choose to give the Lord credit for His divine protection to those who trust in Him.

> The angel of the Lord encamps all around those who fear Him, and delivers them.
>
> —Psalm 34:7

One of our sons was having trouble finding a sense of belonging his freshman year in high school. Oscar and I joined hands and asked the Lord for direction for him. While we were praying, I had a mental picture of two ducks putting their bills together and lifting a little duck into a pool of water.

The accompanying thought was how overjoyed the duckling felt to be in his element. Of course, we suggested to our son to go out for the swim team, which he did. Afterward, he would often remark how good the water felt, especially on hot days. The camaraderie of a team was exactly what he needed.

My first experience at what I later learned was travailing in the Spirit occurred one morning during my prayer time. An almost unbearable sorrow came over me as great cries of anguish came from deep within my spirit. The sobbing shook my whole body; I continued to pray in the Spirit for several minutes. When this lifted, I asked the Holy Spirit to please reveal what had occurred. Instantly, there was a mental picture of two boys in our children's school; their parents were going through a divorce. The Holy Spirit had given me new insight and empathy for the dear children who, as a result of divorce, suffer such agonizing pain.

> For the LORD God of Israel says that He hates divorce…
>
> —MALACHI 2:16

A similar instance occurred while praying for very dear friends who were contemplating divorce. During intercession in the Spirit, the following scene unfolded: The husband was speaking at a light-colored podium on a stage with navy, velvet drapes in the background. His wife and two small sons were seated near him. The smaller son stood as a beam of light shone on him. The older son then stood and began to play a guitar. The father motioned for the mother to come to him and he put his arm around her giving her a hug. Above the couple hung a cross with the bowed head of Jesus dripping blood from His crown of thorns on them. After seeing that, I was most encouraged, especially since we were planning to visit them in another state soon. I took a book about the Holy Spirit and was eager to pray with them. When we arrived, the situation was worse than I had ever imagined. The hostility and anger expressed by the husband and wife to each other was heartbreaking. Before we departed, while the children were outside playing, I shared my desire to pray with them. They became enraged, asking who I thought I was to think I could pray for them. With Holy Spirit boldness, I told them if they would get on their knees and ask Jesus to be Lord of their lives, everything could change. The wife asked how I dared to judge them. I shared that we are to judge by the fruit of God's Holy Spirit, and I didn't see love, joy, peace, or patience there, but that it was available for the asking. The man angrily left the room and the woman glared at me with such hatred it was frightening. We departed with heavy hearts; they were totally closed to hearing the good news of healing through Jesus and the power of His Spirit. Later they experienced a dreadful divorce. Interestingly, the older son did begin to play guitar. When questioning the Lord about what I had seen regarding this couple, the thought came that He allowed me to see what He had planned for them, but they chose their own destructive path.

> For I know the thoughts that I think toward you, says the LORD, thoughts of peace and not of evil, to give you a future and a hope.
> —JEREMIAH 29:11

Years ago, when praying in the Spirit, a mental picture came where I seemed to be looking down through the open roof of a large cathedral. People were coming from every direction. Upon entering, they walked by twos to the front and paused; some went up several steps where a brilliant figure laid hands on them. Instantly, they became small and began to rise up out of the church. Fascinated, I watched as others chose not to ascend to the shining figure. They remained tall and exited through arched doors, back out into the world. I continued to pray and ask the Holy Spirit for an explanation as to what I had seen. Right away the thought came that unless we become as little children we will not enter the kingdom of heaven. I randomly opened the Bible and began to read:

> Assuredly, I say to you, unless you are converted and become as little children, you will by no means enter the kingdom of heaven. Therefore whoever humbles himself as this little child is the greatest in the kingdom of heaven.
>
> —MATTHEW 18:3–4

This was very sobering since more than half the people I had seen chose to stay in the world rather than humble themselves to be prayed over to enter the new realm as a little child. In John 3:3, Jesus tells Nicodemus, "Most assuredly, I say to you, unless one is born again, he cannot see the kingdom of God."

During a Love and Praise prayer meeting we were praying in the Spirit for a local high school, and one lady had a mental picture of what looked like Jesus walking across the campus. He stopped on the football field and dropped to His knees. With His head in His hands, He appeared to be weeping. We prayed, asking the Lord to pour out His Spirit on our schools and to remove the many idols and false gods found there.

At Christmastime one year our Thursday group had been praying for protection for our children and their schools. Later, a friend was telling us of the miracle that happened at our school. One day the children were having an extra practice for the Christmas Program to be held that evening and were dismissed later than usual. Because of this, they were able to avoid what could have been a dreadful tragedy. Someone had had a heart attack while driving their car and ran the stoplight at the edge of campus. They drove into the very place where the students would have been waiting for their rides.

> I will say of the LORD, "He is my refuge and my fortress;
> My God, in Him I will trust."
> —PSALM 91:2

A friend called to inquire if I would be in charge of a lunch program at our school. I prayed about it, asking guidance from the trusted Holy Spirit. Opening my Bible, I began to read:

> It is not desirable that we should leave the word of God and serve tables.... but we will give ourselves continually to prayer and to the ministry of the word.
> —ACTS 6:2, 4

During prayer, I was impressed that there would be many who could help with a lunch program but few willing to spend time in prayer and the study of His Word. I returned the call to say I would not be able to take on the lunch program. I then remembered the saying that we feed our bodies three big meals a day but feed our spirits one little snack on Sunday and wonder why we have so many problems.

Another mental picture came when our Love and Praise Group was praying for more of the Holy Spirit's gifts. I saw a large, white, filigreed, double gate nearly over-flowing with beautifully wrapped presents. In asking the Holy Spirit what that meant, the thought occurred that God longed to open those gates and bestow His many blessings on each of us, but our hearts were not prepared to receive them. Our focus needed to be on the Giver and not on the gifts. We were admonished to seek the fruit of the Spirit which "is love, joy, peace, longsuffering, kindness, goodness, faithfulness, gentleness, self-control" (Gal. 5:22–23). By working on these, we would become more like Jesus since these are all attributes of His character. Conviction came on each of us to work more diligently toward becoming Christ-like so as to draw others to the Lord of lords. Someone remarked how the birds always go for the ripest fruit and that should be an incentive for us to strive to produce the best fruit possible to draw others to God's kingdom.

> By this all will know that you are My disciples, if you
> have love for one another.
>
> —JOHN 13:35

One day, when in deep intercession, I suddenly saw myself walking toward a magnificent, light-colored house. Going up several steps to a large veranda with beautiful, hanging plants, unlike any I had ever seen, I went toward the open door. Upon entering, my eyes were instantly drawn to a shimmering white staircase on my right; it looked as though it was made of mother-of-pearl and appeared to be suspended in mid-air. Glancing down I could see into a transparent, gold-colored floor and wondered if it was made of glass. Everything was pristine and sparkling clean. I walked to a large window frame without glass in it where I saw a glistening lake with two white swans swimming toward me. In a flash, I was back in my room still on my knees, inquiring of the Holy Spirit as to what I had just seen. An almost audible voice said: "I have given you a glimpse of your eternal home." The awesome presence of God and joy in my spirit was indescribable. My heart thrills at the very thought of it!

Many years later during a powerful prayer meeting, while everyone was praying in the Spirit, I had a mental picture of the same large house, only from a distance. A man and little girl were sitting on the step and rose to enter, hand in hand. In my spirit I felt it was Oscar and Mary Bernadette. I was flooded with God's love, peace, and excitement at the thought of joining them someday.

Six months after Oscar went Home I was attending a retreat, and had gone to the main speaker for prayer. I was greatly blessed as she prayed, proclaiming the Spirit of the Lord would give me the oil of joy for mourning, and the garment of praise for the spirit of heaviness, especially since she knew nothing of my recent widowhood and aching heart.

> The Spirit of the Lord God is upon Me...to comfort all who mourn...to give them beauty for ashes, the oil of joy for mourning, the garment of praise for the spirit of heaviness...
>
> —Isaiah 61:1–3

As she prayed for me, I fell under the power of the Holy Spirit and was overcome with the sweet presence of the Lord. In my mind's eye I had a flash of Oscar excitedly saying, "Oh, Joan, just wait till you see this place!" He looked as though he was in his mid-twenties. The joy and awesomeness of that experience has blessed me beyond measure.

Mother had a dream of Oscar after his Home-going in which he took her by the arm, saying he wanted to show her the magnificent flower gardens there. When she told me about this, I shared how he had often remarked to me, after our move to California, that she and Dad should visit in the summer so Mother could enjoy the flowers here. He knew how she loved flowers of any kind and had her yard full of them. Their visits always occurred during the winter months so as to escape the Midwestern cold weather.

Every summer or fall I flew to Iowa to visit my parents. My last visit with Dad was a sad one; when saying good-bye, he wouldn't let go of my hand. I almost canceled my flight, but knew it would be the same the next day since he always dreaded my going. A few days after returning home, I had a dream in which I saw two men walking toward each other. Right away I recognized Oscar. He looked exactly as I had seen him that time at the retreat. Oscar was rapidly walking toward another man but I couldn't make out who he was. Suddenly, I recognized Dad from his walk and from pictures I'd seen of him in his twenties. He was no longer an elderly man of almost ninety-six and in a wheelchair. Instead, he was briskly walking toward Oscar where they embraced with a big bear hug. I woke up with a knowing in my spirit that Dad would be going to heaven soon. When I called Mother to share this, she said Dad had been saying he was so lonesome. She too felt Jesus would be coming for him soon, which He did.

It was always heartbreaking to see how fearful Dad was of dying. He dreaded the thoughts of purgatory and clung to the teaching that he would never be good enough to get right into heaven. In spite of his constant praying, there was the nagging fear that he had not done enough. Again and again, I would share what Saint Paul had written: "For by grace you have been saved through faith, and that not of yourselves; it is the gift of God, not of works, lest anyone should boast" (Eph. 2:8–9). I would ask him if he believed what Saint Paul wrote. About that time, he would take my Bible and check to see if it was the Catholic version, which I always made sure it was. Then, I would ask him what he thought about Jesus saying to the thief on the cross: "Assuredly, I say to you, *today* you will be with Me in Paradise" (Luke 23:43, emphasis added). He just couldn't understand how I was so sure I'd go to heaven and thought perhaps I was committing the sin of presumption. I assured him I could never be good enough to go there on my own; I was going in through faith in Jesus having died on the cross for me.

> I am the door. If anyone enters by Me, he will be saved...
>
> —John 10:9

By accepting this free gift, it was like having my ticket for heaven to hand to the Father, in appreciation for sending His Son Jesus to make the ultimate sacrifice for me.

> My sheep hear My voice, and I know them, and they follow Me. And I give them eternal life, and they shall never perish; neither shall anyone snatch them out of My hand.
>
> —John 10:27–28

> And this is the testimony: that God has given us eternal life, and this life is in His Son. He who has the Son has life; he who does not have the Son of God does not have life. These things I have written to you who believe in the name of the Son of God, that you may *know* that you have eternal life, and that you may continue to believe in the name of the Son of God.
>
> —1 John 5:11–13, emphasis added

This was an ongoing frustration that caused me great sadness. I saw my dad's worry, fear, and concern as he chose his tradition over the Word of God.

For laying aside the commandment of God, you hold
the tradition of men...

—Mark 7:8

There is no fear in love; but perfect love casts out fear,
because fear involves torment.

—1 John 4:18

Dad had prayed many times asking God to forgive his
every sin and invited Jesus to be his Lord and Savior, so I just
had to trust God understood his heart.

...For the Lord does not see as man sees; for man looks at
the outward appearance, but the Lord looks at the heart.

—1 Samuel 16:7

I frequently encounter the same fear and uncertainty
when visiting the sick and elderly. (I am a member of the
Pastoral Care for my church.) In one instance, I asked a dear
friend, who was dying of cancer, if she was eager to see Jesus.
With all the strength her eighty-five pound frame could mus-
ter, she struggled to raise her head. Her eyes were full of fear;
she asked me not to talk like that as she fell back on her pillow. She was still planning to cruise around South America.
She died two weeks later. Another lady was talking about her
deceased husband and planned to be with him in the cem-
etery. I told her he was probably getting her mansion ready
in heaven when she asked me to change the subject, saying
she didn't like to talk about heaven. She passed away several
months later. I have tried to tell several people how much God
loves them and what His Word says heaven will be like. Sadly,
there appears to be no desire to talk about the Lord or interest
regarding eternal life. Some of these people are in their nine-
ties and it can't be very long before they meet their Maker. My

heart aches for them to know Jesus and have a relationship with their loving Savior; they would then be eager to be with Him for eternity.

Several years ago, a neighbor came to tell me his wife had been diagnosed with cancer. I went right over, and seeing how bad she looked, I asked if I could pray with her. She was very open to prayer. I had her repeat after me a simple prayer, asking God to forgive every sin she had ever committed and inviting Jesus into her heart to be her Lord and Savior. We then asked Jesus to fill her with His Holy Spirit. She prayed with great conviction and began to weep saying she had never been much for church. I gave her a couple of pamphlets full of God's encouraging Word. The next day I went to see how she was. With a big smile on her face, she remarked she didn't know what kind of prayer we prayed the day before, but for the first time in her life she couldn't stop praying. It was thrilling to see the peace of God all over her and realize she was a new creature in Christ.

> There is therefore now no condemnation to those who are in Christ Jesus...
> —ROMANS 8:1

The following week her husband called to say she had just expired while sitting in her favorite chair. I ran over immediately! In spite of his sorrow, he commented on the wonderful peace she had and was most grateful. A few years later, I was able to pray with him. He also had an encounter with his Redeemer before he slipped into eternity.

I like to compare learning about heaven to experiencing the beauty of Hawaii. Once we saw, smelled, and enjoyed the beauty of the islands we could hardly wait to go back. Likewise, if we were taught about heaven, imagine how eager we would be to go there. Instead, people are filled with fear and dread for lack of teaching. The Bible says, "He shall die for lack of instruction, and in the greatness of his folly he shall go astray" (Prov. 5:23). It breaks my heart to hear many say the Book of Revelation shouldn't even be in the Bible. This book even promises a blessing to the reader: "Blessed is he who reads and those who hear the words of this prophesy" (Rev. 1:3). If only one learned what God has prepared for His children, there would be joyous anticipation to be with Him and partake of His goodness.

> Eye has not seen, nor ear heard, nor have entered into the heart of man the things which God has prepared for those who love Him." But God has revealed them to us through His Spirit. For the Spirit searches all things, yes, the deep things of God.
> —1 Corinthians 2:9–10

I love to read in Revelation where God, Himself, will dwell with us. There will be no more tears, death, sorrow, crying or pain (Rev. 21:3–4). The glory of God will illuminate the city and "there shall be no night" (Rev. 22:5). No evil shall be there. This has blessed me more than I can express; joy floods my soul as I meditate on these glorious words.

Never had I been taught about the need to have my name written in the Lamb's Book of Life in heaven. (See Luke 10:20 and Philippians 4:3.)

> But there shall by no means enter it anything that defiles, or causes an abomination or a lie, but only those who are written in the Lamb's Book of Life.
> —Revelation 21:27

And if anyone takes away from the words of the book of this prophesy, God shall take away his part from the

Book of Life, from the holy city, and from the things
which are written in this book.

—Revelation 22:19

To me, this is extremely serious with everlasting consequences.

In June of 1998, my older brother, Paul, called to say he was going to Ireland to vacation and research the family history. He had been offered a Fulbright Grant, along with several other professors, to spend five weeks in Africa during July and August, but didn't think he would go on that trip. Later, I was surprised to get a call saying he couldn't pass up the trip to Africa, since he had never been there and all his fellow professors were going. He already had his shots and was enthused about this new adventure. At the end of the first week of the trip, I received a phone call that Paul had been in an accident. An approaching van had lost a wheel and hit the professors' van head-on. Paul was seated behind the driver and both were killed instantly. This was the first time I had experienced anyone close to us dying so suddenly. Oscar and I always had had a special bond with Paul. After leaving the Trappist monastery, he had lived with us for several years while working on various degrees. In a state of shock, I fell to my knees begging God for a word for my dear, departed brother. Praying in the Spirit, between sobs, I begged God to please speak to me through His Holy Word. Randomly, I opened my Bible and began to read: "I have fought the good fight, I have finished the race, I have kept the faith" (2 Tim. 4:7). The subtitle above verse six read: "Paul's Valedictory." God's Word brought the peace that passes understanding.

And the peace of God, which surpasses all understanding,
will guard your hearts and minds through Christ Jesus.
—PHILIPPIANS 4:7

Later when praying, I opened to the same quote found
in a teaching in the back of my Bible. The night of Paul's wake
a friend of his handed me a prayer Paul had said at a recent
meeting. He had closed with, "May it be said of all of us that
we have fought the good fight, finished the race, and kept
the faith." I was overwhelmed at the blessings of God's con-
firmations. Having attended minor seminary with the Bene-
dictines, and following the rule of St. Benedict when in the
Trappist monastery, St. Benedict was his favorite Saint. Paul
went to heaven July 11, 1998, on the feast of St. Benedict!

Mother was blessed with the beautiful faith of a little
child. She lived to be almost ninety-five and could hardly wait
to be with Jesus and all her loved ones. I called every Sunday afternoon, and her frequent lament was why the good
Lord didn't come and take her Home. I assured her He still
needed those prayers of intercession here on earth for family
and friends to make it to heaven. One day while interceding
for her, I had a strong sense that the Lord was coming for her
soon in June. Longing to be there when Jesus came, I flew
right out to be with her; thankfully, she seemed to improve.
Obviously, I realized I hadn't heard from the Lord correctly,
when Mother was still on this earth in July of that year. Questioning the Holy Spirit about this, I was given the following message: "Do not be anxious for anything, My daughter.
Continue to praise and thank Me for your good mother. She
is in My hands and no evil shall touch her. I alone have power
over life and over death. Trust Me, for My ways are perfect.
Again I say, be not anxious for I have everything under control as you shall see." Mother went to heaven the following

year on June 29, 2002. It was the feast day of Saints Peter and Paul! I'm sure husband Peter and son Paul were there to welcome her, and Oscar was able to show her the gorgeous flower gardens. As usual, my heavenly Father "had everything under control."

> To everything there is a season, a time for every purpose under heaven: A time to be born, and a time to die…
> —ECCLESIASTES 3:1–2

The Communion of Saints becomes more real to me with each passing year. Psalm 97:10 says, "He preserves the souls of His saints; He delivers them out of the hand of the wicked." Psalm 50:5 reads, "Gather My saints together to Me, those who have made a covenant with Me by sacrifice." I am reminded of a time long ago, when a group of us were seated around our table in prayer. I had a mental picture of a circle of bearded, robed men looking down from a balcony, nodding in approval. We all began to smell incense. God's word now comes to mind: "Let my prayer be set before You as incense" (Ps. 141:2). While joining hands during prayer, one by one everyone began to feel a pulsing in our hands. A nurse in the group said it was impossible for all of us to have the same heartbeat. Like little children, we agreed it had to be the heartbeat of the Lord as Head of the body of Christ that we, the members, were experiencing. How we praised and thanked God for the privilege of belonging to Him.

> And He put all things under His feet, and gave Him to be head over all things to the church, which is His body, the fullness of Him who fills all in all.
> —EPHESIANS 1:22–23

CHAPTER 11

Deliver Us From Evil

———◆◆———

AFTER MY HOLY SPIRIT BAPTISM I was amazed and shocked to discover that as real as the Holy Spirit had now become, so, too, was the reality of an evil spirit. I was surprised to read Jesus' words: "You are of your father the devil...he is a liar and the father of it" (John 8:44). In John 8:47, Jesus continues, "He who is of God hears God's words; therefore you do not hear, because you are not of God." How many times I had heard God's Word with my head only, and not with my spirit! (The saying about the longest trip in the world being from the head to the heart seemed to ring true.) Now that the flame of God's Spirit was kindled in me, there was an insatiable hunger for the truth I was finding in His Word.

> However, when He, the Spirit of truth, has come, He will guide you into all truth...
>
> —JOHN 16:13

> Jesus answered, "Most assuredly, I say to you, unless one
> is born of water and the Spirit, he cannot enter the king-
> dom of God. That which is born of the flesh is flesh, and
> that which is born of the Spirit is spirit."
> —John 3: 5–6

I still had great concern as to how one could know for sure that they were born again. When seeking an answer regarding this, the immediate thought came: "Just as a new-born baby hungers for its mother's milk, so one born of the Spirit, hungers for the spiritual food of God's Word."

I now read Scripture as though seeing it for the first time. "When He had been baptized, Jesus came up immediately from the water; and behold, the heavens were opened to Him, and He saw the Spirit of God descending like a dove and alighting upon Him" (Matt. 3:16). "Then Jesus was led up by the Spirit into the wilderness to be tempted by the devil" (Matt. 4:1). He overcame all three temptations by quoting from the Scriptures. (See Matthew 4:1–10.) In so doing, He taught us the power of using the double-edged sword of the Word.

> For the word of God is living and powerful, and sharper
> than any two-edged sword, piercing even to the division
> of soul and spirit…and is a discerner of the thoughts
> and intents of the heart.
> —Hebrews 4:12

It is no wonder the father of lies hates the truth of God's Word. It exposes him and teaches everyone who is interested how to deal with his deception. It is written, "Man shall not live by bread alone, but by every word that proceeds from the mouth of God" (Matt. 4:4). I was becoming very aware of the adversary! One of his main purposes is to keep mankind from knowing about the many blessings and promises the Bible contains. God's Word appears to be the most controversial book ever written. In John 10:10 we read, "The thief does not come except to steal, and to kill, and to destroy. I have come that they may have life, and that they may have it more abundantly." The Holy Spirit was teaching me how to meditate on God's Word and appropriate the blessings therein. In Psalm 1, we read:

> Blessed is the man who walks not in the counsel of the ungodly, nor stands in the path of sinners, nor sits in the seat of the scornful; but his delight is in the law of the LORD, and in His law he meditates day and night. He shall be like a tree planted by the rivers of water, that brings forth its fruit in its season, whose leaf also shall not wither; and whatever he does shall prosper.
>
> —PSALM 1:1–3

Some thirty years ago I attended a class on prayer and learning how to hear from the Holy Spirit; I received a teaching that I use daily. The teacher, a powerful woman of God and author of several Christian books, taught about the three sources we hear from: the Holy Spirit, the evil spirit, and our own spirit.

> Therefore submit to God. Resist the devil and he will flee from you. Draw near to God and He will draw near to you.
>
> —JAMES 4:7–8

She also stressed dying to our own thoughts, so as to open up only to the Holy Spirit who will lead us into all truth. Whenever praying for anyone, I begin with a prayer using this teaching. I acknowledge the importance of submitting to God's Holy Spirit, resisting the evil spirit, and then dying to my own spirit. It is also necessary to ask the Holy Spirit to reveal any sin or lack of forgiveness in one's heart. After waiting on and trusting in the Lord's revelation, then repent of whatever comes to mind; it is like clearing the channel so as to hear only from the One True Source. The enemy of our souls can counterfeit many things; however, he cannot counterfeit the peace of the Holy Spirit. When seeking guidance I pray for the gift of discernment, always checking for peace, or the lack of it, in my spirit. Someone once asked if I wasn't afraid of being misled. I gave her the above teaching and told her my trust was in the Holy Spirit, who promises to lead us in all truth.

> However, when He, the Spirit of truth, has come, He will guide you into all truth.
>
> —John 16:13

> For He Himself has said, "I will never leave you nor forsake you."
>
> —Hebrews 13:5

The best advice I have ever found is to ask the Holy Spirit for a scripture regarding the situation at hand, especially since He watches over His Word to perform it.

> So shall My word be that goes forth from My mouth; it shall not return to Me void, but it shall accomplish what I please, and it shall prosper in the thing for which I sent it.
>
> —Isaiah 55:11

Many years ago, I was frequently awakened in the night by an irregular heartbeat. The family doctor wasn't concerned, stating I just needed more rest. This sometimes became so alarming I considered waking my sleeping husband to call 911. As I continued to pray, the same thought would come: "You shall not die, but live, and tell of the works of the Lord." Wonderful peace would come over me as I drifted back to sleep. One day, while reading in the psalms, I was overjoyed to discover: "I shall not die, but live, and declare the works of the Lord" (Ps. 118:17). No wonder I felt such peace; I was hearing God's Word. I did go to a heart specialist and discovered the cause of my problem was a mitral valve prolapse, for which I now take a small tablet every day.

At a Monday night prayer meeting in the early seventies, a marvelous teaching was given by an elderly Pentecostal pastor, on the cross of Christ and how Jesus' shed blood defeated Satan. We also learned a song about the power in the blood of Jesus, singing it several times. This song went deep into my spirit; I couldn't get it out of my mind and kept humming it. Coming home that night, I noticed a copy of a news magazine that my husband had been reading. On the cover was a picture of Anton LaVey; inside there was a story about his being a high priest of Satan. My heart sank at the thought of him being lost for all eternity, by following the father of lies. As I knelt by our bed finishing my night prayers, I began to pray for Anton. Instantly, I became totally paralyzed; my upraised arms were frozen in place as a force grabbed my throat squeezing so tightly I could barely breathe. Absolutely terrified, my only thought was of the new song I had just learned about the power in the blood and name of Jesus. I made a desperate attempt to speak; struggling with everything in me I tried to whisper the name of Jesus. All I could get out was a *J, Je, Jes*, and finally the blessed name *Jesus* came forth. Immediately, the force left as rapidly as it had come. Trembling all over,

I silently thanked and praised God for the power and protection of His wonderful name. The presence of Jesus then became so strong, I could have spent the rest of the night in praise and adoration to my wonderful Savior and Deliverer.

I didn't wake my sleeping spouse, since he was already concerned that I was becoming a little strange. I did share this with him later. I asked some mature Christians about that frightening experience. They said I probably needed a commission from the Lord to pray for one so sold out to the enemy; they also felt I was no doubt attacked due to being very young in the Spirit. We did rejoice that I had been so well prepared that very evening for such an encounter. I had experienced firsthand proof of the power and safety we have available to us through the name and the blood of Jesus.

> And they overcame him by the blood of the Lamb and
> by the word of their testimony...
> —REVELATION 12:11

Several years later, our prayer group was devastated to learn that the daughter of Anton LaVey was to be a guest speaker at the local Catholic University where our son attended. Some of us got together to pray protection for the students and for God's Holy Spirit to bring conviction on the professors for allowing such darkness on campus.

> This is the message which we have heard from Him and
> declare to you, that God is light and in Him is no darkness at all. If we say that we have fellowship with Him,
> and walk in darkness, we lie and do not practice the
> truth.
> —1 JOHN 1:5–6

A similar attempt to snuff out my life happened sometime later. Awakened from a sound sleep, I felt an evil presence in the room accompanied by a horrible stench, much like that of stagnant water in a vase of rotting flowers. The next thing I knew, a force was on my chest with what felt like hands around my neck, choking me. The most hateful eyes I had ever seen glared at me as the grip tightened on my throat. Frozen with fear and the hair standing up on my arms, I gasped trying to speak the name of Jesus. Once I could call out Jesus' name, the horrible presence left as suddenly as it had come. Shaking uncontrollably, I asked the Holy Spirit what had happened. The immediate thought was that the spirit of death had tried to ensnare me, but the name of Jesus had sent it away. It was very reassuring to once again experience the omnipresence of God and the power in the name of Jesus.

> Therefore God also has highly exalted Him and given Him the name which is above every name, that at the name of Jesus every knee should bow…
>
> —Philippians 2:9–10

> Be sober, be vigilant; because your adversary the devil walks about like a roaring lion, seeking whom he may devour. Resist him, steadfast in the faith, knowing that the same sufferings are experienced by your brotherhood in the world.
>
> —1 Peter 5:8–9

John G. Lake, a missionary to Africa, stresses in his book, *The John G. Lake Sermons*, the power and protection that are available to all who believe and put faith in the Spirit of Christ Jesus.[1] He was ministering where the bubonic plague was raging. Doctors asked what he was using to keep from getting the plague. He shared his belief that as long as he kept his soul in contact with the living God, so that His Spirit was flowing into his soul and body, no germ could attach itself to him for the Spirit of God would kill it. He then asked the doctor to do an experiment by putting foam that came from lungs of the dead under a microscope; there they saw masses of living germs staying alive for some time. Then filling his hand with the foam and placing it under a microscope they watched as the germs died instantly. The doctor asked for an explanation whereby John said: "That was the law of the Spirit of life in Christ Jesus. When a person's spirit and body are filled with the blessed presence of God, it oozes out of the pores of one's flesh and kills the germs." In Isaiah 53:5 we read:

> But, He was wounded for our transgressions, He was bruised for our iniquities; the chastisement of our peace was upon Him, and by His stripes we are healed.

There is a mighty resource of untapped Holy Spirit power available to those who believe.

> My people are destroyed for lack of knowledge.
> —HOSEA 4:6

After an attempt was made on President Ford's life, there was a picture in a magazine of him encased in a bulletproof bubble. The question followed as to whether that was what would be necessary to protect our leaders. In viewing that picture, I had the thought that the protection offered to all who believed in the power of God's Holy Spirit, through the precious blood of Jesus, was a thousand times greater than the protection of a bulletproof bubble.

A manifestation of God's deliverance happened the night I came from the hospital after hysterectomy surgery. I was feeling very discouraged and experiencing much anxiety. While praying, I felt as though three sets of chains physically fell from me. Asking the Lord for an explanation, the thought came that I had been set free from the chains of fear, anxiety, and doubt.

> For God has not given us a spirit of fear, but of power and of love and of a sound mind.
>
> —2 TIMOTHY 1:7

Long ago, I heard David du Plessis, known throughout the world as "Mr. Pentecost," speak on the unimaginable power and love of Jesus Christ. I was startled to hear him say that Jesus was so all-loving He even answered the devil's prayer. With his Bible open, he began to read: "So they [demons] begged Him [Jesus] that He would permit them to enter them [swine]. And He permitted them" (Luke 8:32). He also spoke on the necessity of being born again. "Most assuredly, I say to you, unless one is born again, he cannot see the kingdom of God" (John 3:3). He told about being in prayer during a lengthy plane ride when the thought had come to him: "God has no grandsons." Puzzled, he questioned the Holy Spirit as to what that meant. He felt the Lord's answer was that each person comes to God of his or her own free will, and not merely as a result of being born into a believing family. David continued to speak about the love of God and the power of praying for our families and friends to be born again. He stressed that sometimes even deliverance was necessary for people to attain eternal life. I hung on every word and was especially blessed when he said no one could snatch us from the Father's hand once we had *truly become His sheep.*

> My sheep hear My voice, and I know them, and they
> follow Me. And I give them eternal life, and they shall
> never perish; neither shall anyone snatch them out of
> My hand.
>
> —JOHN 10:27–28

I am reminded of an incident that happened many years later. A call came from a frantic mother whose daughter had tried to commit suicide for the third time. My answer for every situation was and is to go before the Lord to seek His wisdom and direction. It is always comforting to realize when we do not know how to pray, the Spirit Himself makes intercession for us:

> Likewise the Spirit also helps in our weaknesses. For we
> do not know what we should pray for as we ought, but
> the Spirit Himself makes intercession for us with groan-
> ings which cannot be uttered.
>
> —ROMANS 8:26

Much of the night was spent in prayer, using the keys of the kingdom which are to bind and to loose, as Jesus tells us in Matthew 16:19. My prayer was to bind and cast to the foot of the cross the forces of the enemy that come to rob, kill, and destroy, according to John 10:10, and to loose the power of the Holy Spirit on this lovely young girl as found in Acts 1:8. During intercession, I had a mental picture of a man dressed in black straddling the world while playing a guitar; pink pigs were coming from under the earth, passing through his legs, and then scattering across the globe. The following morning, I called to inquire how things were and asked if the daughter listened to much music. The mother replied her daughter put headphones on the minute she woke up and continued to listen to her music even when in the car going to school. I shared the mental picture I had received during prayer. We wept and prayed together binding all lyrics pertaining in any way to suicide, and also that she would destroy those tapes, in the name of Jesus. To my knowledge she did change what she listened to and never tried suicide again. She has grown up to be a beautiful, prayerful woman of God.

Later, at one of our prayer meetings, someone brought an article exposing the back masking that was being done on music records. This was a new concept to most of us. When I shared it with our college-aged son, he became quite indignant remarking that it sounded like some fanatic Christian writer. Weeks later my younger brother and nephew came to visit. Our nephew, to our surprise, had recently heard a former disc jockey, turned Christian, speak on the very subject. It was indeed dangerous since words and messages were recorded backwards on a soundtrack preventing one's mind from rejecting them. To prove his point, my nephew asked our son to put a record on the turntable and use the eraser end of a pencil to turn the record backwards while the needle was down. To everyone's horror, words like "take the mark, don't be afraid," "the number is 666," "serve Satan," "Satan is god," etc. could be heard. That was proof enough for our son. He destroyed most of his records, however, he did save a couple and attempted to share what he had learned with college friends; they thought he had gone fanatical and turned a deaf ear. I then read Jacob Aranza's *Backward Masking Unmasked*,[2] Bob Larson's *Rock*,[3] and Steve Lawhead's *Rock Reconsidered*,[4] which further exposed the deception of the great deceiver and father of lies.

> How you are fallen from heaven, O Lucifer, son of the
> morning! How you are cut down to the ground, you
> who weakened the nations! For you have said in your

> heart: "I will ascend into heaven, I will exalt my throne
> above the stars of God; I will also sit on the mount of
> the congregation on the farthest sides of the north; I
> will ascend above the heights of the clouds, I will be like
> the Most High."
>
> —ISAIAH 14:12–14

Reading about the fall of Lucifer as a result of his pride and rebellion, one can easily recognize rebellion as a central theme in rock music. Also, I learned that perhaps Satan was a great musician in heaven. (See Ezekiel 28:13–17.) The name *Lucifer* means *light bearer*. St. Paul writes: "For Satan himself transforms himself into an angel of light" (2 Cor. 11:14). Jesus says, "I saw Satan fall like lightning from heaven. Behold I give you the authority to trample on serpents and scorpions, and over all the power of the enemy, and nothing shall by any means hurt you" (Luke 10:18–19). It is interesting to see how often a lightning bolt is used as a symbol of Satan.

Currently, the lightning bolt is the prominent mark used on Harry Potter's forehead in the popular Harry Potter series. The titles alone, proclaiming schools of sorcery, should cause one to realize these books are contrary to God's Word. The following scriptures *forbid sorcery* even stating those who practice it will not enter heaven: Exodus 22:18, Deuteronomy 18:10, Jeremiah 27:9, Malachi 3:5, Acts 13:8, Galatians 5:20, Revelation 9:21, 18:23, 21:8, and 22:15. In reading and marking the first three Potter books, I was amazed at the subtle ways in which evil was portrayed as being good.

> Woe to those who call evil good, and good evil; who put
> darkness for light, and light for darkness...
>
> —ISAIAH 5:20

One wonders whether there would be an outcry over books about schools of murder, adultery, and fornication or would they also be considered appropriate for little children, due to their popularity, and on every "must read" list? Recently, I read where the occult is on the rise in England, crediting the famous *Harry Potter* books. It is interesting to note the author, J. K. Rowling, is now listed as one of the world's billionaires. The god of this world must be pleased! Have we become the proverbial frog in the kettle staying in the murky water until it gradually turns to the boiling point?

> My people are destroyed for lack of knowledge.
> —HOSEA 4:6

A frustrating episode occurred many years ago when our schoolchildren brought home ads for the Church Spring Luncheon. A prayer partner and I made an appointment with one in authority to request a different speaker. We were met with mocking laughter at our concern over a speaker who, in Deuteronomy 18:10–14, God forbids. We were informed that that person speaking with us also had a ticket and planned to attend. With heavy hearts, we remained in prayer during the time of the luncheon. Few ever recognized the dreadful fallout from that day. One by one, stories of tragedy were told about people who sought answers from a source displeasing to our Lord, thus opening a door for their destruction.

> The thief does not come except to steal, and to kill, and to destroy.
> —JOHN 10:10

In her book, *Defeated Enemies*, Corrie Ten Boom tells the story of a young soldier guarding his post on a dark night.[5] He made a wrong turn into the enemy camp, was captured, and became their prisoner. No amount of explaining or begging allowed for his freedom. Any one of us can become ensnared in the enemy's trap, especially if we are unaware of his many deceptions. The good news, however, is that there is always victory when one has been taught how to fight the good fight of faith, using the double-edged sword of God's Word. "Your word is a lamp to my feet and a light to my path" (Ps. 119:105). Our heavenly Father's Ten Commandments are like loving signposts on the map of life, there to guide and protect us as we travel the narrow road. (See Exodus 20:2–17.)

I once had a terrifying dream in which I was standing on top of a high cliff where I could see crowds of people, beautifully dressed as though going to a New Year's Eve party. They were singing, cheering, and raising champagne glasses as they walked down a massive stretch of highway. From my vantage point, I could see beyond the sharp curve ahead; the road was out and everyone would fall into the ocean. I began to scream for them to turn back. I even seemed to have a megaphone so I frantically yelled into it for them to stop because the road was out, but to no avail. Many would laugh and wave, shouting I was an alarmist and other words to that effect. Not one person turned around! No words could express my frustration; I continued to scream as I watched these unsuspecting people fall into eternity. I woke up in a sweat with my heart pounding; the dream had been so real. I prayed for the Holy Spirit to enlighten me as to its meaning. The answer seemed to be in the thought, "Enter by the narrow gate; for wide is the gate and broad is the way that leads to destruction, and there are many who go in by it" (Matt. 7:13). Recalling this brings great sadness, since no one would listen to what I was so desperately trying to tell them to save their lives.

The thought of anyone being lost, perhaps for all eternity, is almost beyond comprehension.

I am reminded of another dreadful dream in which I was walking along a stream when I noticed a newborn baby flailing in the water. I ran over and snatched the little one up and then began to panic as dozens of tiny babies, and pieces of bodies, came rushing down the then blood-red water. Once again there was such a feeling of helplessness; I woke up horror stricken with an accelerated heart rate. I prayed for the many mothers who had fallen into another of the devil's lies, thinking it is their right to slaughter the holy innocents and label it abortion.

> Even so it is not the will of your Father who is in heaven
> that one of these little ones should perish.
>   —MATTHEW 18:14

When praying for women who have had an abortion, it is heart-wrenching to see the suffering they frequently have been through. After sharing the love their heavenly Father has for them and leading them in a prayer of repentance, it is nothing short of miraculous to watch the freedom in the Holy Spirit come over them. In some cases, the enemy of their souls has held them in the bondage of guilt for many years. One touch from the divine Comforter often totally sets them free as they realize God sent His Son to forgive all our sins.

> Bless the LORD, O my soul, and forget not all His benefits: who forgives all your iniquities, who heals all your diseases, who redeems your life from destruction, who crowns you with lovingkindness and tender mercies...He has not dealt with us according to our sins, nor punished us according to our iniquities. For as the heavens are high above the earth, so great is His mercy toward those who

fear Him; as far as the east is from the west, so far has He removed our transgressions from us.

—PSALM 103:2–4, 10–12

I heard someone say that God buries our sins in the sea of forgetfulness and we should put up a sign that reads: "No Fishing!"

A darling little boy, who used to accompany his mother to the Love and Praise Prayer meetings, would curl up with his blanket under our buffet and take a nap. One day his mother asked prayer for him; she was very concerned over his recent nightmares. When he took off his jacket, I noticed he had a large picture of ET on his shirt. She commented that that was his pajama shirt which he loved to wear. Inquiring when the nightmares started, it was evident they coincided with his new pajamas. Interestingly, there were no more nightmares after prayer, and the ET pajama shirt was replaced. In the movie ET, this hideous-looking creature was given god-like qualities as it touched and healed the little boy, depicting a scene much like Michelangelo's painting of God's finger touching Adam, the first created man.

Do not be deceived, God is not mocked...

—GALATIANS 6:7

Years later, after the prayer group had moved to another home, we were praying for the mother-in-law of the hostess. In the Spirit, I saw a little, dark brown, demon-like figure that reminded me of ET. Using a short, dark brown croquet-type mallet, it was furiously hitting the older woman we were praying for in the hip. The hate in its eyes matched the evil I had seen the night I was being choked by a similar type demon. It disappeared as we rebuked the spirit of infirmity and arthritis, commanding it to go to the foot of the cross in the name of Jesus of Nazareth. The dear lady stood up and touched her hip in the very place where the enemy had been hitting her; she was overjoyed that the pain had completely gone. We had a great time of praise and thanksgiving for God's goodness and mercy.

> Behold, I give you the authority to trample on serpents and scorpions, and over all the power of the enemy, and nothing shall by any means hurt you.
> —LUKE 10:19

Luisa, the new leader of this group, did missionary work with her husband. On one occasion when visiting her family in Guam, she was told about a little, second-grade niece who was having nightmares and had become terrified of going to school. Questioning the small girl, it was discovered that the nun preparing the children for first communion was teaching them Silva Mind Control. She was using guided imagery, asking the children's spirit-guides to teach the little ones. Obviously, she was unaware that these "spirit-guides" were actually demons. She was even getting into astral projection, which involves out-of-body experiences; no wonder the little child was so fearful. The missionary tried to expose this to the clergy, but there was no response. After coming home, Luisa wrote a letter to Rome detailing the dangers of this being taught in a Catholic school or to any children. We all laid hands on that letter and prayed for God to intervene. The cardinal in charge was notified, and Silva Mind Control was no longer allowed to be taught to the little children in Guam. Oh the blessings of one committed person who follows the Word of God!

Therefore if the Son makes you free, you shall be free
indeed.

—John 8:36

Many times our home was visited by Jehovah's Witnesses.
They were dear, sincere people bringing their doctrine and
trying to teach their interpretation of their Bible. I learned a
lot by studying to have answers for them; they were very well-
versed in Scripture. On one occasion they gave me a Bible.
I was impressed to compare the Gospel of John with their
version as I prayed for the Holy Spirit to lead me in all truth.
There was a discrepancy in the very first sentence. It read: "In
the beginning was the word and the word was with God and
the word was a god." My version read, "In the beginning was
the Word, and the Word was with God, and the Word was
God." (See John 1:1.) My Bible clearly stated that Jesus is
the Word and the Word WAS God, not simply a god. I read
the entire chapter of John marking the many differences as I
went. The following week I tried to return their Bible showing
the discrepancies but they wouldn't take it. I wanted to give
them some of my literature to read, which was also refused.
I desperately tried to share about the Holy Spirit who would
lead them in all truth, but their minds were closed due to
their own agenda. When they realized I was not a candidate
for their beliefs, they stopped coming to our home. Not long
after this, a lady in the Love and Praise prayer group brought
a friend who was visiting from another part of the state. She
asked prayer for her son and his wife who were considering
joining the Jehovah's Witnesses. I gave her the freshly marked
Bible requesting they check the Gospel of John alongside their
Bible. One of the greatest truths I have learned is to see what
others do with Jesus.

He [Jesus] said to them, "But who do you say that I am?" Simon Peter answered and said, "You are the Christ, the Son of the living God." Jesus answered and said to him, "Blessed are you, Simon Bar-Jonah, for flesh and blood has not revealed this to you, but My Father who is in heaven.

—MATTHEW 16:15–17

Jesus said to him, "I am the way, the truth, and the life. No one comes to the Father except through Me."

—JOHN 14:6

Nor is there salvation in any other, for there is no other name under heaven given among men by which we must be saved.

—ACTS 4:12

The above scriptures give me great comfort when confronted with: "There are many ways to God." I have been accused of being narrow-minded, bigoted, and unloving by quoting these verses. The greatest gift to give anyone is the truth that will lead them to heaven! What a sad commentary on our loving heavenly Father to send His only Son to die for us, if there was another way in.

For God so loved the world that He gave His only begotten Son, that whoever believes in Him should not perish but have everlasting life.

—JOHN 3:16

It is our responsibility to obey the great commission of Jesus:

Go therefore and make disciples of all the nations, baptizing them in the name of the Father and of the Son

and of the Holy Spirit, teaching them to observe all
things that I have commanded you; and lo, I am with
you always, even to the end of the age.
                              —Matthew 28:19–20

Many years ago I attended a class dealing with moral-
ity. One participant asked what the speaker thought about
young people living together without being married. The
theologian/teacher replied that if they were in love, then it
was okay. My hand shot up to ask what about God's commandment, to which another lady remarked they weren't
committing adultery. The speaker quickly moved on before I
had a chance to read:

> Do not be deceived. Neither fornicators, nor idolaters,
> nor adulterers, nor homosexuals, nor sodomites, nor
> thieves, nor covetous, nor drunkards, nor revilers, nor
> extortioners will inherit the kingdom of God.
>   —1 Corinthians 6:9–10

> For this you know, that no fornicator...has any inheri-
> tance in the kingdom of Christ and God.
>   —Ephesians 5:5

After class, a friend asked how I could believe in the
Bible. I told her I had just received a letter from my mother
telling about a terrible Midwestern snowstorm; I didn't call
the weather bureau to see if she was telling the truth for I
trusted her word. If I could trust my mother, I certainly didn't
have trouble trusting the Word of God. She teased me saying
I sounded like a Bible-thumper. Ironically, a few years later
this same lady asked me to please pray for her. She had been
diagnosed with cancer and felt I was the only one she knew
that seemed to have a hotline to heaven. There was such a

feeling of compassion and God's love for her as we prayed. Hopefully, the scales have been removed from her eyes and she is now learning the truth of God's Word firsthand, in His presence.

> For now we see in a mirror, dimly, but then face to face. Now I know in part, but then I shall know just as I also am known.
>
> —1 CORINTHIANS 13:12

CHAPTER 12

Aglow

———◦•◦———

OSCAR ANSWERED THE DOOR ONE SUNDAY afternoon to find a lovely lady asking if Joan Galli lived here. Informing her she had found the right place and inviting her in, Oscar called me from the other room. I came out to meet someone who would play an important role in my ongoing journey with the Lord.

Kim and her family had recently moved to the area. At her daughter's school, she had met my friend Gail, who suggested she contact me; she told Kim we "talked alike." The two of us sat on the couch sharing the wonders of our heavenly Father for over two hours. After she left, Oscar asked who she was. I replied that it was the first time we had met but there was an instant rapport and feeling of kinship in the Lord.

Some time later, Kim called saying she wanted to stop by to ask a big favor. Upon arriving, she informed me there was to be a Women's Aglow Chapter in our town. (This is an international, nondenominational, women's organization that leads people to faith in Jesus Christ). She had been asked to be the local president and when praying about a vice president, my name kept coming to mind. We prayed together, and I told her I would continue to pray regarding the vice presidency and of course check with my husband.

Just a month prior to this, a prayerful woman of God named Dottie was praying for me when she began to prophesy that I would be involved in Women's Aglow. I laughed and told her I didn't even attend the meetings. It was her turn to laugh as she continued to prophesy, stating not only would I attend, but I would someday be the president. I thought she had missed it on this, even though earlier, she had gained my full attention when she asked if the name Oscar meant anything to me. Another friend and I began to chuckle. Dottie asked what was wrong; in unison we told her that was my husband's name. She gave a sigh of relief saying she almost didn't speak that name since the only Oscar she knew of was Oscar Mayer hot dog. Dottie admonished us to obey the voice of the Lord no matter how strange it may seem and then gave us a teaching on the gift of prophesy.

> Therefore, brethren, desire earnestly to prophesy, and do not forbid to speak with tongues.
> —1 Corinthians 14:39

> Let no corrupt word proceed out of your mouth, but what is good for necessary edification, that it may impart grace to the hearers. And do not grieve the Holy Spirit of God, by whom you were sealed for the day of redemption.
> —Ephesians 4:29–30

Dottie was legally blind and confined to her home. This dear elderly saint of God had been a night nurse and now felt called to take the night watch in intercession. Frequently, she would phone with a word of encouragement or a teaching she had received in prayer. One morning she called asking, "What is the matter with your mother? I kept interceding for her last night." The previous day, I had received a call that mother was quite ill and needed gall bladder surgery. I was very touched and blessed that the all-knowing God of the universe would have her interceding for my precious mother. God continued to bless us through this powerful prayer warrior. He used Dottie mightily the night I called her after Oscar's visit from Jesus, when Oscar said he wanted to go Home. The wisdom and insight the Lord gave her was a turning point for all of us and especially for me, to die to self and let God have His way. I miss Dottie greatly since her Home-going, but know she is now enjoying her eternal reward.

> His lord said to him, "Well done, good and faithful servant; you were faithful over a few things, I will make you ruler over many things. Enter into the joy of your lord."
> —Matthew 25:21

Oscar had given his wholehearted approval to my joining Aglow. It had been two or three years since the Love and Praise Prayer Group had met in our home and he knew how I missed working with the women. When I told him about Dottie's prophecy, he just grinned and suggested I obey the Lord's call.

Little did I realize the important role this organization, with the motto "Be Aglow and burning with the Spirit" would play in my life. (See Romans 12:11, AMP.) The godly women involved have also experienced the fullness of the Holy Spirit and are not ashamed to operate in His wonderful gifts.

For I am not ashamed of the gospel of Christ, for it is the power of God to salvation for everyone who believes...
—ROMANS 1:16

Aglow women stand in awe at the spiritual, mental, and physical manifestations our heavenly Father displays through His signs and wonders. Many hurting women come to the meetings in need of prayer, and leave having experienced a wonderful touch from "Abba Father."

And because you are sons [and daughters], God has sent forth the Spirit of His Son into your hearts, crying out, "Abba Father!"
—GALATIANS 4:6

The Aglow local, national, and international retreats continue to play a significant role in my spiritual walk. At the international conferences, with thousands in attendance, one of the highlights is the "Parade of Flags." Women in their native costumes march into the convention hall carrying the flag of their country. The flags are then displayed on the enormous stage throughout the retreat. Aglow is presently operating in 164 countries. Many women comment on this being a foretaste of heaven.

For all nations shall come and worship before You...
—REVELATION 15:4

Blessing and honor and glory and power be to Him who sits on the throne, and to the Lamb, forever and ever!
—REVELATION 5:13

There is rarely a dry eye in the hall, as people begin to feel the powerful presence of our Lord Jesus. Everyone recognizes that only the Holy Spirit of God could bring such amazing unity among women from the many diverse denominations and nationalities.

> I do not pray for these alone, but also for those who will believe in Me through their word; that they all may be one, as You, Father, are in Me, and I in You; that they also may be one in Us, that the world may believe that You sent Me.
>
> —JOHN 17:20–21

I am reminded of the wonder I first experienced, over thirty years ago, when attending similar meetings in the large Catholic Retreat Center. My heart thrilled at the love and unity of Christians brought together by the Holy Spirit. The focus was not on doctrinal differences; the focus was on Jesus and His Word.

> …and there will be one flock and one shepherd.
>
> —JOHN 10:16

I did accept the vice president position for Aglow and, four years later, the prophecy given through Dottie came true. Kim was asked to be on the Area Board and I was installed as president of our local chapter. Later, when our board was lining up speakers for the monthly meetings, we couldn't find one for the month of September. During prayer regarding it, the thought came that I was to be the speaker. I remembered reading in the Word that one should not promote oneself, so I kept silent.

> For not he who commends himself is approved, but whom the Lord commends.
>
> —2 CORINTHIANS 10:18

Shortly after at a board meeting, Jane informed us that when in prayer she had a strong impression that Joan was to be the September speaker; the others agreed. I then shared my confirmation, never imagining what was to transpire since this was the month of April or May.

In July, Oscar was diagnosed with pancreatic cancer. With all these godly women praying, I had great faith he would be healed, even trusting I could share his miracle in my September talk. I had experienced firsthand God's healing of my back, varicose veins, and bone spurs in my heels, plus all the miraculous healings I'd seen in others through the years. My faith remained high as I continued praying the many scriptures for healing and believing in the Lord's mercy. Our sons later voiced their concern that I wasn't facing reality by my insistence on God's miracle for their dad. How I praise and thank God for the Holy Spirit's comfort and continual guidance. Everything fell into place when I let go and let God have His way. The scripture that sustained me during those days and following was:

> And He said to me, "My grace is sufficient for you, for My strength is made perfect in weakness."
> —2 Corinthians 12:9

As stated in chapter nine, Oscar went to be with the Lord on August 28, 1991, three weeks before his sixty-first birthday. Due to Labor Day weekend, the funeral was held on September 3rd, our oldest son's birthday. With the help of the Holy Spirit, I did speak for the Aglow meeting three days after the funeral. I shared how Oscar had indeed received his "miracle of total healing." It was certainly not the way I had planned, but there was great peace in knowing my wonderful husband was enjoying his "Glory Day." He was in the presence of his beloved Lord and Redeemer and all his loved ones; he now had the perfect healing. I, too, had received a miracle in learning to hear from and trust in God's plan to do things His way.

> Every word of God is pure; He is a shield to those who put their trust in Him.
>
> —PROVERBS 30:5

Aglow became a lifeline during this time in my life. Because I was in charge, I was forced to attend the many meetings, get the flyers out each month, pray for the numerous requests on the prayer chain, and continue to stay active. When I was a child I longed to have a sister, and now I was blessed with dozens of loving, caring, godly sisters. There was no time to retreat from doing the Lord's work or to ever indulge in a pity party, for which I am most grateful.

> I will bless the LORD at all times; His praise shall continually be in my mouth.
>
> —PSALM 34:1

The next few years were extremely difficult. The selling of my husband's share of the company after his death was very painful due to unforeseen circumstances. The Lord's grace was once again sufficient, as He provided me with the godly wisdom, discernment, and strength of our oldest son.

> Behold, children are a heritage from the LORD, the fruit of the womb is a reward.
>
> —PSALM 127:3

The following summer, I flew to Iowa to help my parents. They could no longer stay in their home since they both needed extra care. It was a sad time for all of us as we sorted through and dealt with the many treasures accumulated over sixty years of marriage. Dad, at age ninety-three, was very unhappy at leaving his home to go to a nursing facility, but thank God Mother was flexible. I had often suggested they move to sunny California, but they both insisted their roots were too deep with church, family, and friends in the Midwest. Fortunately, my brother and his wife were able to get them into one of the best homes in the state.

Returning from a very stressful week with my parents, I helped our middle son prepare for his flight to the east coast, where he was scheduled to attend graduate school. Two weeks later, our youngest son also flew to the east coast for college; he departed on the second anniversary of Oscar's death. After a whirlwind of activity, sickening nausea came with a vengeance as we left the airport; full realization hit me that I would be alone for the first time in my life. Our oldest son was very concerned. He and his wife begged me to stay at their home, but I knew this was something I'd have to work through sooner or later.

> The Lord will command His lovingkindness in the daytime, and in the night His song shall be with me.
> —Psalm 42:8

Entering our now silent and empty house, I begged my Lord for fresh revelation and strength from the blessed Holy Spirit, His divine Comforter.

> Blessed be the God and Father of our Lord Jesus Christ, the Father of mercies and God of all comfort, who comforts us in all our tribulation, that we may be able to comfort those who are in any trouble, with the comfort with which we ourselves are comforted by God.
> —2 Corinthians 1:3–4

I praise and thank God for my wonderful family and also for my many Aglow sisters; He continues to use each one to help me "Be Aglow and burning with His Spirit."

> And my God shall supply all your need according to His riches in glory by Christ Jesus.
>
> —PHILIPPIANS 4:19

Through the years I have remained active in Aglow by serving on a local board and then the area board. Once again, I am on a local board. I still consider it a lifeline. The contacts made through this organization will last through eternity.

My fervent and constant prayer is for another great move of the Holy Spirit to ignite a hunger in God's dear people for the truth of His wonderful Word. Also, I pray that multitudes will "become as Little Children," so as to enter the Kingdom of God.

> At that time the disciples came to Jesus, saying, "Who then is greatest in the kingdom of heaven?" Then Jesus called a little child to Him, set him in the midst of them, and said, "Assuredly, I say to you, unless you are converted and become as little children, you will by no means enter the kingdom of heaven. Therefore whoever humbles himself as this little child is the greatest in the kingdom of heaven. Whoever receives one little child like this in My name receives Me."
>
> —MATTHEW 18:1–5

> Let everything that has breath praise the LORD. Praise the LORD!
>
> —PSALM 150:6

Epilogue

F OR SOME TIME, THERE HAS BEEN a knowing deep within my spirit that I was to write and share the many truths and blessings I have experienced since receiving the baptism of the Holy Spirit. The thoughts of writing a book became more frequent even upon being awakened in the night. I decided to seek a confirmation.

My friend Jane and I attended a wonderful prayer meeting where I asked a Spirit-filled lady to please inquire of the Lord regarding a confirmation for me. Looking puzzled, she asked what about; I told her that was what I wanted the Holy Spirit to reveal to her. Bowing her head she began to pray. Soon she looked up and said, "You won't laugh if I tell you what I saw, will you?" I assured her I would not laugh. She proceeded to say she had had a mental picture of me sitting at a desk, writing; I got up and walked to a window as if being inspired and then sat down and began to write again. Her next question was, "Does that mean anything to you?" I then shared the reason for my request and we agreed the meaning was very clear. We were both thrilled to have received such a direct answer and together we praised and thanked the Lord for the wonderful manifestation of His Holy Spirit.

> For everyone who asks receives, and he who seeks finds, and to him who knocks it will be opened.
> —Matthew 7:8

Once I believed that writing this book was a commission from my Lord, I took it seriously and began to obey. At that point, the thoughts and memories literally flowed forth. Encouragement came from family and friends and I gained strength from repeating, again and again, the following scripture:

> I can do all things through Christ who strengthens me.
> —Philippians 4:13

The desire of my heart is that God will be glorified through this humble writing and that many others will be inspired to also write and share the blessings of the Holy Spirit in their lives. All the Master needs is a yielded vessel.

> …as the clay is in the potter's hand, so are you in My hand…
> —Jeremiah 18:6

Praise You Father, Praise You Son, Praise You Holy Spirit, Three in One!

Notes

CHAPTER 2
ADDED BLESSINGS

1. *Good News for Modern Man* (New York: American Bible Society, 1966).

CHAPTER 3
LOVE AND PRAISE DAYS

1. Norman Williams and George Otis, *Terror at Tenerife* (Van Nuys, CA: Bible Voice, 1977), 63–64.

CHAPTER 4
PRAYER GROUP CHALLENGES

1. Bob Larson, *Larson's Book of Cults* (Wheaton, IL: Tyndale House, 1982), 92.

CHAPTER 6
THE HOLY SPIRIT CLASS

1. Dennis Bennett, *The Holy Spirit and You* (Gainesville, FL: Bridge-Logos Publishers, 1994).

CHAPTER 10
HOLY SPIRIT MANIFESTATIONS

1. Mitch Pacwa, S.J., *Catholics and the New Age* (Ann Arbor, MI: Servant Publications, 1992), 220–221.

CHAPTER 11
DELIVER US FROM EVIL

1. Gordon Lindsay, *The John G. Lake Sermons* (Dallas, TX: Christ for the Nations, 1979), 108.

2. Jacob Aranza, *Backward Masking Unmasked* (Shreveport,

LA: Huntington House, 1983).

    3. Bob Larson, *Rock* (Wheaton, IL: Tyndale House Publishers, 1980).

    4. Steve Lawhead, *Rock Reconsidered* (Downers Grove, IL: Inter-Varsity Press, 1981).

    5. Corrie Ten Boom, *Defeated Enemies* (n.p.: Christian Literature Crusade, 1962).